AHA Moments

in

TALENT MANAGEMENT

A Business Fable
With Practical Exercises

Mark Allen

ASTD Press is an internationally renowned source of insightful and practical information on workplace learning, training, and professional development.

ASTD Press
1640 King Street
Alexandria, VA 22314

Ordering information: Books published by ASTD Press can be purchased by visiting ASTD's website at store.astd.org or by calling 800.628.2783 or 703.683.8100.

Library of Congress Control Number: 2014944295

ISBN-10: 1-56286-916-7
ISBN-13: 978-1-56286-916-8
e-ISBN: 978-1-60728-426-0

ASTD Press Editorial Staff:
Director: Glenn Saltzman
Manager, ASTD Press: Ashley McDonald
Associate Editor: Sarah Cough
Editorial Assistant: Ashley Slade
Cover Design: Marisa Kelly
Text Design: Bey Bello

Printed by Versa Press, Inc., East Peoria, IL, www.versapress.com

Introduction

In some books, the first line is memorable ("It was the best of times, it was the worst of times…"). In others, it's pithy ("Howard Roark laughed."). The first line of this book sums up its underlying philosophy and provides its raison d'être: "People are our most valuable asset."

The line is spoken by Will Perez, the CEO of the fictional company Capital View, which is the setting for this book. Like so many CEOs, Perez spouts this cliché without giving it much thought. Executives at almost all organizations profess that people are their most valuable asset, but do all of these organizations actually behave as if it were true? In many cases the answer is no. That paradox is what this book is dedicated to addressing and, I hope, resolving.

Everyone says that people are their most valuable asset and many actually believe it. However, very few organizations have talent practices that reflect a true belief in the value of people. In a few cases, it might be because they don't really believe in the value of their talent. More often, the inattention to talent is due to a lack of understanding of how to truly manage talent to unleash its value. On top of this, many organizations are handcuffed by policies and procedures that have been inherited from the last century (or, in some cases, the century before that). In short, we are managing organizations in the Talent Age using principles handed down from the Industrial Age. While this might be a problem for some organizations, I view this as a tremendous opportunity for those organizations that can effectively manage talent.

In *Strategy-Driven Talent Management*, Rob Silzer and Ben Dowell define talent management as, "an integrated set of processes, programs, and cultural norms in an organization designed and implemented to attract, develop, deploy, and retain talent to achieve strategic objectives and meet future business needs." The burgeoning field of talent management is intended to help organizations make better decisions about the most effective ways to maximize the value that can be derived from the talented employees it can attract and employ.

The ability to develop an "integrated set of processes" has proven to be challenging due to the large and complex nature of our organizations and because most companies have not focused on talent in an organized and integrated manner. Those organizations that have successfully developed effective talent management programs and procedures have a distinct competitive advantage. This book is intended to help organizations understand how to focus on talent and develop effective talent practices.

The setting for the book is a fictional company. All of the characters are fictional. However, all of the events are based on real cases. Every story related in these pages is based on actual organizational practices that I have witnessed or had described to me. Most of the scenarios are not based on isolated incidents—they are stories that have been repeated time and time again.

As you read this book, you may find that many of the characters and events seem familiar. That is by intent. Many of the practices described here are commonplace. At times you might even think the story is based on your own organization (and it's entirely possible that it is). So even though the setting is fictional, the practices described in the story are very real. And, most importantly, the Talent Management Principles presented by the story's protagonist are best practices used by organizations to combat the ineffective and counterproductive talent practices that plague many organizations.

And so I prefer to define Talent Management more simply. To me, Talent Management is a series of practices managers use to maximize the value from an organization's most valuable asset—talented people.

HOW TO USE THIS BOOK

I hope you enjoy the stories in this book. But more than that, I hope you find them useful. If you feel that some of the practices described in this book are descriptive of your organization, think about whether they are actually helping or hindering. And if they are a hindrance, give some thought as to what you can do to change things. If the events of a chapter are unfamiliar, think about what you can do to help your organization avoid some of these pitfalls.

At the conclusion of each chapter, there are two groups of questions for you to consider. The first set is an Organizational Assessment. These questions ask about the talent practices that are currently in place in your organization. You are asked to determine the extent to which your organization employs certain practices. If you tend to agree with a statement, your organization is doing well regarding that practice. However, if you find yourself giving a lot of scores of 1 or 2 in response to the Organizational Assessment questions, then your organization probably has some practices in place that do not effectively manage talent. This can be a call to action.

The other set of questions are Reflection Questions. These open-ended questions are about you. As people have shared with me stories of their organization's practices, they frequently do so with a mixture of frustration and helplessness. If you're not the CEO or chief people officer of your organization, perhaps you're not in a position to make sweeping policy changes. However, you are probably in a position to do something. So the Reflection Questions ask about your own personal practices and, most importantly, about what you can do. Many of these questions ask specifically about what actions you can take regarding the Talent Management Principle described in the preceding chapter. I encourage you to think about these questions and take action.

I believe I am required by international law to have at least one quote from Peter Drucker in a book like this, so here it goes: "The ability to make good decisions about people represents one of the last reliable sources of competitive advantage, since so few organizations are very good at it." This was true when Drucker wrote it more than 50 years ago and it is still true today. And therein lies the opportunity for readers of this book.

It is my sincere hope that after reading this book, you will have figured out some actions you can take to help your organization unleash greater value from its talent, achieve its goals, and gain the competitive advantage that Drucker described over a half-century ago.

P eople are our most valuable asset."

Maria Green laughed. She had just asked Will Peres, the CEO of Capital View, what his organization's most valuable asset was. She knew what his answer would be before she asked the question. She had asked this question to every CEO she had ever met and their answer was always the same. They must teach them that on the first day of CEO school, she mused. The question was harmless enough and the answer had become a cliché, but Maria moved ahead with her follow-up question, the one CEOs really didn't like.

"So how much of your time do you spend on your greatest asset?"

Peres paused for a moment before answering. Was Maria genuinely interested in knowing his honest answer, or was she testing him? He wondered. It was a fair question, so he'd give her an honest answer, but one that might test her a bit.

"Not as much as I should. But that's why I need a strong executive to head up HR."

Again, it was the answer she had expected. CEOs always claim that their greatest asset is their people, but usually confess that they don't spend enough time on that asset. In Maria's view, they spent far too much time focusing on the financial assets. Of course, the financial assets are only earned by the good work of talented people. That's why Maria had gone into HR in the first place. When she got her MBA from Columbia Business School, many of her classmates just rode the subway down to Wall Street and went to work in finance. Now Maria found herself on Wall Street, but she was interviewing for the top HR job with a global financial consulting firm.

She had heard good things about Will Peres. While he was a Wall Street lifer, he had a reputation of being open to new ideas. Maria thought she could work with him. She had some concerns about some of the other senior executives she had met during the interview process at Capital View, but after a couple of interviews she was starting to like Will. She felt he liked her as well, and she thought that today's interview—her third with Will—was going to result in an offer. But before she made her decision about whether to accept, she decided to test Will one more time.

"So if people are the greatest asset at Capital View, do the executives of this organization behave on a day-to-day basis as if that were true?"

It was Will's turn to laugh. Now he knew she was testing him. He was the CEO, she was, at this point, just an applicant, but she was asking the tough questions. He admired her spunk. He liked spunk. So let's see how she reacts to some honesty, he thought.

"No, we don't."

"Then I'm not sure this is the right company for me."

"It's the right company for you if you're up for a challenge. I'm convinced that our only source of competitive advantage is our people. But as you suspected, we haven't behaved that way as an organization, and I'm just as guilty as anyone. We need someone to keep us on the right track. We need an HR executive who will push us to be more people-focused. And I think you could do that for us."

"Is this an offer?"

He liked her directness. He was convinced she would be good for Capital View. "Yes, I'd like to offer you the position. Assuming we can agree on a compensation package."

So there it is, she thought. He wants to hire her. But she would only take the job under the right circumstances. She had two more tests for Will.

"Will, I don't want to have a long negotiation about money. I know what this job should pay, and if you agree, then we have a deal." She took out a small memo pad, wrote something on a piece of paper, folded it in half, and slid it across the desk. She knew this was overly dramatic, but she wanted to make her point.

Will laughed out loud. "I thought people only did that in movies." He had to admit, she was different. Will prided himself on knowing what everyone on Wall Street earned and he knew what he should be paying for this job. And he knew that she knew what these jobs paid, so he was pretty sure she wouldn't be over asking here. As he unfolded the paper, he was pretty sure he knew what the number would be.

He was genuinely surprised at what he saw. It wasn't a number at all. It was letters.

"I don't understand. What does this mean?"

Maria had written three letters on the page: CFO.

"It means I want to be paid the same as you pay your CFO."

"But you don't even know what he makes."

"No I don't, but I think I should be paid the same as you pay him."

"Maria, you should understand that the pay scale for CFOs is different from that of vice presidents of HR. If you look at the annual report of virtually any publicly traded company, you'd see that the CFO always makes more than the VP of HR."

"I know. This is precisely the reason why I'm asking you to pay me what you pay your CFO."

"Maria, I like you and I want to hire you, but I just can't pay that kind of money."

"Why not?"

"It's just not done."

"Why isn't it done?"

Will paused. It was a fair question and one he didn't have an answer for. Besides, this was supposed to be a job offer and a compensation negotiation, not an interrogation. So he decided he would start asking the questions.

"Maria, let's back it up a little. How much did you make on your last job?"

"That's irrelevant. The question is, what is this job worth at this company?"

"I think I'm willing to pay a fair price. Let me make you an offer." He decided he would use her trick and pulled out his pen and a sheet of paper.

"Don't bother."

Will was shocked. She didn't even want to see his offer? "Why not?"

"Because this isn't a negotiation. I will only work for you if you pay me what you pay the CFO."

Now he was exasperated. "But you don't even know what that number is. I was prepared to make you a very generous offer. It might even be more money than you suspect our CFO makes."

"I'm not trying to be difficult here, but this isn't at all about the amount of money." She had set her trap, and now she was about to spring it. Let's see if he'll put his money where his mouth is, she thought.

"Will, you said that your greatest asset is your people. If you really meant it, then there's no reason why you shouldn't be willing to pay the executive who oversees that asset as much as you pay the executive who oversees the financial assets."

She had a point, Will thought. Why did they always pay CFOs more? The short answer was that CFOs expected a big number and VPs of HR were willing to work for less. But maybe they were willing to work for less because that's all the market would bear. The longer answer was that Maria was right. Organizations tend to value CFOs more than VPs of HR because they really do focus more on money than people. He thought about the money for a moment. He could certainly afford to pay her what he's paying Bobby. But boy, would he be pissed off! Will smiled at the thought of his CFO finding out that the new head of HR would be making as much as he was. It was funny, but he didn't relish that inevitable conversation. It really wasn't the money that was the issue here, it was the precedent. As Will reflected on the potential ramifications, he realized that Maria was just staring at him and not saying anything. She had made her point and was waiting for his response.

"But Maria, Bobby's been a CFO for a number of years and…"

"And I've headed up HR for a number of years."

"Look, I understand your point. But it's a big number…"

"And we both know you can afford it."

"Would you be willing to consider…"

Maria cut him off again. "Will, I don't mean to interrupt, but I want you to know that this is not a negotiation. I would not be willing to consider any other terms. We always say, 'Our greatest asset is our people,' but we don't mean it. If you really mean it, you would be willing to pay your people person as much as your money person. If I were to accept anything less, we would be sending the message that people aren't as important. So if I were to take this job, I would only do it if we were serious about people being our most important asset. I believe you meant it when you said you wanted an HR executive who would push the company to be more people-focused. Well, now's your chance to take that first step."

"Don't you even want to know what his salary is?"

"Nope."

"Wait a minute, you're willing to take the job and you're not even curious about the money?"

"I'm sure Bobby is well compensated. But this isn't about the money. It's about the message we're about to send."

He admired her conviction. He also couldn't help but notice the confidence behind her use of the first-person plural pronoun. Plus, she made a good point. She was different and they needed someone different. He knew having Maria would shake things up a bit, and they needed that. At least, it would never be boring.

"All right, Maria, I'll give you the same compensation as the CFO has. Do we have a deal?"

"Well, actually there is one more thing."

Uh-oh. He just made her the highest paid vice president of human resources that he had ever known and now she's asking for something else?

"We need to talk about the title."

This isn't so bad, Will thought. Titles are cheap and I'm willing to negotiate. "Your predecessor was the vice president of human resources. Given this conversation and your compensation package, I'd be willing to change it to senior vice president of human resources."

Maria said, "That's not what I was going for." She pulled out her pen and another piece of paper.

"For the love of God, Maria, please don't slide another piece of paper across my desk!"

They both laughed. "Fair enough. Will, I want my title to be chief people officer."

Will was surprised. Maria didn't seem like the type to care too much about titles. He knew she would end up getting her way, but he wanted to find out a bit more about how she thinks.

"It's not really a traditional title in financial services. Why do you want it?"

"Because it's what the job is."

"Isn't the job senior vice president of human resources?"

"First of all, 'people' is a simpler, more descriptive term than 'human resources.'

Our employees are people—they don't think of themselves as resources that happen to be human. More importantly, 'human resources' and 'HR' are terms that have taken on a negative connotation. People think of HR as some sort of internal policing agency that only shows up when there are problems."

"OK, so why not senior vice president of people?"

"What do you call the person in charge of money?

"Chief financial officer."

"How about the person in charge of marketing?"

"Chief marketing officer."

"Technology?"

"The chief technology officer. I get it, I just didn't think you were the kind of person who cared about titles."

"I don't care about the title per se. But if all of those people are chiefs, shouldn't the person in charge of your organization's greatest asset also be a chief? Anything less, and you'd be sending the message that the people department is less important than the other departments."

She had a point. His company, like most, had paid lower salaries to HR and afforded the department less status than the others. He had never really thought about it before, but he was sure he was going to be hearing a lot more about these issues from Maria. He was confident she would be good for the organization.

"OK, you've got it—chief people officer it is. I shudder to ask, but is there anything else?"

"No, that's it…" And then, smiling, she continued, "for now."

They both knew there would be more discussions like this. Maria added, "Will, I really want to thank you for both giving me this opportunity, and for being open to some of the ideas I've been sharing. To be honest, even though the money and the title aren't that important to me, I wouldn't have taken the job if you hadn't agreed to give me the same status as your other senior executives. In order for me to be successful in this job, the message we send about people is vitally important, not only to me, but to the future of the company."

"Maria, you've obviously got some strong ideas about the people part of an organization."

"I do. As a matter of fact, I call them Talent Management Principles. They are fundamental principles that are the key to the success of any organization. And yet in my experience, even though most people would agree with the underlying concepts, most organizations don't practice them."

"OK, I'll bite. What are these principles?"

"The first principle is what we have just discussed here today."

Talent Management Principle Number 1
People are your organization's most valuable asset.
Behave as if you believe this to be true every day.

She was right. Ever since he had become CEO, he had probably said that people are his most valuable asset more than 100 times. But he had to admit that Capital View did not behave as if that were true. He knew he had managers who treated people as replaceable commodities, not valuable assets. He also knew that he personally had focused more on the financial aspects of running the business than on the people side and when he and Bobby discussed expenses, they always viewed people as costs, not assets.

"OK, Maria, that's a good one. What are the rest?"

"I think we've had enough for one day. I'll hold off on sharing my other Talent Management Principles until I actually start the job." She gave him her best grin.

"I really look forward to hearing the other principles." He genuinely meant it. However he wasn't sure how these principles—and his new chief people officer—would be received by some of his employees.

"Maria, I have a feeling I can count on you to keep me on my toes and to shake things up around here."

You have no idea, Maria thought to herself. Just wait.

Organizational Assessment

	NOT AT ALL		NEUTRAL		TO A GREAT EXTENT
1. How frequently does your organization say that people are its greatest asset?	1	2	3	4	5
2. Does your organization behave every day as if it truly believed that people were its greatest asset?	1	2	3	4	5
3. Does your CEO spend a significant amount of his or her time on human capital issues?	1	2	3	4	5
4. Does your organization compensate its senior human resources executive or chief people officer at a level comparable to the other senior executives?	1	2	3	4	5
5. Does your organization give its senior human resources executive or chief people officer respect, status, and prestige comparable to the other senior executives?	1	2	3	4	5
6. Does your organization tend to talk about people as assets as opposed to costs?	1	2	3	4	5

Questions for Personal Reflection

1. Was there anything described in chapter 1 that seemed descriptive of your organization?

2. What can you do to ensure that your organization behaves on a daily basis as if it truly believes that people are its greatest asset?

3. What can you do to help ensure that people are viewed as assets instead of costs?

2

O n Maria's first day on the job, she attended her first executive team meeting. She had met each of the members of the executive team during the interview process, but today was her first meeting as a member of the team. She had some thoughts about how each member of the team might react to her ideas, but she was keeping an open mind and hoped that they would all be receptive.

Will Peres opened the meeting. "I'd like to officially welcome Maria Green as our chief people officer."

Maria wondered how her new title would be received. She also suspected that Bobby Rawlings, the CFO, knew that she was making as much as he was. His full name was Robert Randolph Rawlings III. People affectionately called him "R Cubed." His family had been on Wall Street for generations and his grandfather had been the president of the New York Stock Exchange. Maria had expected stuffiness and formality, but he had welcomed her warmly at their first meeting and had asked her to call him Bobby. She thought he might have some objections to her title, her compensation, or the shift to a talent mindset that she was going to be proposing. She looked apprehensively at Bobby, but he just smiled at her. The trouble came from across the table.

"What kind of title is that?" asked Karen Michaels, the chief operating officer. One of the most powerful people in the company, Karen was in charge of the company's consulting division.

Maria's first thought was, how am I going to answer this? The answer "very carefully" came to her. It was her first executive team meeting and she didn't want to start off confrontationally. Should she go through her routine of asking what titles the other chiefs have? While she was pondering this, she heard a friendly voice from the head of the table.

"It's one that I think is perfectly appropriate for the job she has." Will to the rescue! Maria's respect for Will just went up a few points.

Will continued, "As you're about to hear, Maria and I have some ideas about changing the ways we view talent in this company."

"What's wrong with the way we've been running things before she got here?" It was Karen again.

Maria waited for Will's response, but this time he was looking at her. It was time for her to start sharing her views on talent. Maria knew she had to tread carefully. "I'm sure there's nothing wrong. But let me ask all of you this, do you think you have been leveraging the talent in this organization to achieve the maximum possible value?"

She looked around the room. Will was smiling. Bobby was looking over at Karen, awaiting her answer. The other two members of the executive team, Regina Clark, the chief marketing officer, and Dave Marx, the chief technology officer, were also silent and looking at Karen for her response.

Karen employed one of her favorite tactics, answering a question with a question. "What are you implying?"

"I'm saying that people are the greatest asset in this company, wouldn't you agree?" She looked around the room, but didn't wait for any answers before continuing. "I believe that we have the opportunity to leverage even greater value from our people than we have in the past. Wouldn't you all agree that it would be beneficial to this company if we could accomplish that?"

It was Bobby who answered. "As CFO, I'm all about creating value," he said smiling, "but I think we've been pretty good at managing our people. We certainly work them hard enough. I'm not sure we could squeeze any more value out of them."

Maria knew where to go with this. "I'm not talking about working them harder. As a matter of fact, that might be part of the problem. I've looked at a few numbers. We've got some pretty significant turnover in certain parts of the company." She didn't look at Karen, but she was referring to the consulting division. "Our employee engagement measures also aren't where I'd like to see them. And I've noticed that a lot of our employees are not taking advantage of the training and development opportunities that we offer."

Karen jumped in. "I can address that one."

Of course you can, thought Maria.

"Let me explain to you how our business works," Karen said. "Our consultants bill for their time. When they are working for a client, they generate revenue. When they are sitting in a classroom, we are paying them, but they're not generating revenue. Our managers are encouraged to have their consultants deliver as many billable hours as is humanly possible. That's how this company makes money."

"Thanks for the lesson, Karen," Maria managed to say without a hint of sarcasm in her voice. "The problem, as I see it, is our managers."

Karen responded defensively, "I can tell you with great certainty that in our consulting division, our managers are getting maximum output from their consultants."

"That's precisely the problem. By pushing them so hard, we are burning them out. That's why we annually have double-digit turnover among our consultants."

"Hey, this is a Darwinian world we live in. Those who can't cut it should be culled from the herd."

"I've looked at the turnover. It's not just the numbers, it's who we've been losing. We're not losing those who can't cut it, we're losing some who don't want to cut it. Many of the consultants with the highest performance reviews are leaving. I believe our managerial practices are driving away some of our best people. We're replacing them, in some cases, with less experienced, less effective consultants. Even more importantly, we're spending an inordinate amount of time hiring and training new consultants. There is a real cost to this and I think we have an opportunity to eliminate a lot of this turnover by refocusing our managers."

"Are you suggesting that our managers focus on something other than maximizing the output of their employees?"

Maria realized that the meeting had devolved into a debate between her and Karen. The rest of the team was watching intently. Maria knew this was her first test and she had better pass.

"Yes, that's exactly what I'm suggesting."

As smugly as possible, Karen asked, "OK Chief People Officer, tell me, what do you think is more important for our managers to focus on than maximizing output?"

Maria was ready for this one. "I think the job of the manager is to hire the right people, develop their skills and knowledge, keep them engaged in their work, and retain them within the company."

"That's all well and good, but we only make money when our consultants are out there billing…"

"And I think the best way to maximize billings is to hire talented consultants, train them well, keep them engaged in their work, and keep them employed in this company. If we get those things right, we're not only bound to have lots of billable hours, but we'll also have satisfied clients." Maria had made sure to hit on this point, as client satisfaction scores had been slowly dropping. Maria knew that some long-standing clients were starting to become perturbed at the turnover among consultants.

Karen was fuming. "Now wait just a minute. Are you accusing…"

Will finally interrupted, "No one is accusing anyone of anything. We certainly have been encouraging our managers to push their consultants to maximize billable hours. And we certainly have seen a high level of turnover. And exit interviews indicate that burnout is one of the prime reasons for departure. Frankly, I've been uncomfortable with this for a while. All of us in this room are workaholics, but I don't think all of our employees want to live and breathe company business. We say this is a company that encourages work-life balance, but we don't really mean it. We pay lip service to work-life balance because it sounds good, but we push our employees until they drop."

Karen spoke to Will a little more calmly, "So are you suggesting that we lower our goals for revenue generation?"

Maria intervened, "I think we can achieve the same goals—or higher ones—in a different way."

"Go on." Karen seemed genuinely interested.

"I think that by refocusing our managers on hiring the right people, developing them appropriately, keeping them engaged, and retaining them, we are bound to get good results, wouldn't you all agree?"

Everyone was nodding, so Maria pressed her advantage. "If you agree that these are important managerial priorities, to what extent do you think managers should be held accountable for accomplishing these talent-related functions?"

Will jumped in, "I'm not sure I understand the question."

"I guess what I'm asking is, what percent of a manager's time—and what percent of a manager's accountability—should be based on hiring, developing, engaging, and retaining talent?"

Karen was the first to respond, "OK, I get it. I suppose about 20 percent sounds right."

Regina went next, "Maria's made a good point here. I think it should be higher. I'll say 30 percent"

Dave smiled, "I'll go to 40!"

Bobby was laughing, "I hate to be outbid—50 percent!"

Maria got caught up in the moment, "What if it were 100 percent?"

Karen brought them back to earth, "That's insane. We can't have managers ignoring their other responsibilities. Are you really suggesting 100 percent? That would never fly."

"You're probably right, it would never fly," Maria conceded. "But think about it. If managers spent 100 percent of their time ensuring that they hired the right people, developed their skills, and kept them engaged and employed, wouldn't we be just about guaranteed to get good results?"

"Maybe, but that's not realistic."

"Fair enough, but I would suggest that the percentage should be at least 50 percent. That would send the message that this is the most important part of a manager's job."

"Makes sense to me." Bobby was the first to chime in.

Maybe the CFO won't be the obstacle I thought he would be, thought Maria.

The rest nodded their agreement, so Maria continued. "We've all agreed that managing talent should be the most important part of a manager's job. Perhaps more than 50 percent. So let me ask this: At our company, today, to what extent are managers held accountable for hiring, developing, engaging, and retaining talent?"

"I can tell you that in my division it's no more than about 10 percent." It was Regina, the head of marketing.

"That sounds about right," said Dave.

Karen went next, "In the consulting division, it's probably zero."

Will took over. "Wow. It appears we have a pretty big disconnect. We all agree that managers should be focused on making sure we have the right talent in place and keeping that talent engaged and employed. But we don't hold them accountable for this. As a matter of fact, we hold them accountable for a lot of other things, some of which might end up being a bit counterproductive."

"What do you suggest?" Karen was all business now.

Will turned to Maria, "Maria, will you take this?"

"I think we need to communicate to our managers that their job is not just to deliver results. The job of the manager has always been to manage the resources of the organization. And since the greatest resource the company has is people, then the most important aspect of their job is talent management—specifically the functions of hiring, developing, engaging, and retaining talent."

"So are we telling them that results are no longer important?"

"Of course not. I think we, as an executive team, need to send the message that the best path to achieving results is through the effective management of talent."

Will added, "I think Maria's right. And I think that the problem so far has not been that our managers have been doing things wrong, I think it's that we have been sending our managers the wrong message. So moving forward, I think it's up to us to start sending the right message. Can we all agree?"

Maria looked around the room. Everyone was nodding. She wasn't sure if it was based on the case she had made or the team's respect for Will, but one way or another, they had made some real progress today.

Will continued, "I want to thank Maria for bringing these issues to our attention today and for changing our thinking a bit. As you might have gathered, Maria has some pretty strong ideas about issues relating to people. She calls them Talent Management Principles, and I suspect what we've talked about today is one of them. Maria?"

"Thanks, Will."

Talent Management Principle Number 2
The most important job of a manager is to oversee
the talent in an organization. The best way to
achieve results is to hire, develop, engage, and
retain good people.

Will looked around the room at his executive team. They looked thoughtful, but exhausted. When he hired Maria, he knew she would shake things up a bit at Capital View. So far, she had lived up to his expectations. He wondered, with just a tiny bit of apprehension, what would be next.

Organizational Assessment

	NOT AT ALL		NEUTRAL		TO A GREAT EXTENT
1. To what extent does your organization leverage its talent to maximize value?	1	2	3	4	5
2. Does your organization proclaim that work-life balance is a priority for its employees?	1	2	3	4	5
3. Does your organization behave as if it truly values work-life balance for its employees?	1	2	3	4	5
4. Does your organization tell its managers that it is important for them to hire, develop, engage, and retain talent?	1	2	3	4	5
5. To what extent does your organization hold managers accountable for hiring, developing, engaging, and retaining talent?	1	2	3	4	5
6. In general, do you believe the managers in your organization are effective managers of talent?	1	2	3	4	5

Questions for Personal Reflection

1. Was there anything described in chapter 2 that seemed descriptive of your organization?

2. What can you do to ensure that your organization's stated position on work-life balance matches the reality?

3. If you are a manager, what percent of your time do you spend on the talent practices of hiring, developing, engaging, and retaining the right people?

4. If you are a manager, to what extent are you held accountable for talent practices? What do you think it should be?

5. What can you do to minimize the disconnection between what you believe about how managers should be held accountable for talent practices and the way they are currently held accountable?

Maria had stepped outside for lunch. There was a hot dog vendor on the street around the corner from the Capital View building. Although she usually tried to eat a healthy lunch, she had a weakness for hot dogs. New York City hot dog vendors had those special onions in red sauce that you just couldn't get anywhere else. Maria had a yearning today, plus she wanted to get out of the office and have some alone time. She didn't think her fellow executives would be lunching on street meat, so she figured she could have a few minutes alone to digest the morning's events.

That morning, she had gotten into a bit of an argument with Will about her desire to hire Tom Washington as the company's chief learning officer. Tom was an award-winning chief learning officer who was well-respected throughout the financial services industry as well as the world of corporate learning. Maria had just learned that Tom was on the job market and she wanted to snap him up.

Capital View had a training department, but Maria had wanted to grow it into a full-fledged corporate university. While the training department had a good reputation for delivering training classes, Maria wanted to expand it into an entity that could develop people in numerous ways beyond what was offered in training classes. Capital View's training director was good at overseeing training programs, but Maria needed an executive who was experienced at managing the learning and development function for a large organization. Tom Washington was just the person for the job.

The problem was, when she approached Will about hiring Tom, the CEO had put the brakes on. He told her that Capital View's procedures dictated that she write a job description for the position, get budgetary approval, post the position, and then have the position open and available for applications and interviews for a minimum of 10 business days before she could make an offer. Maria knew that this process would take at least a month and that an executive like Tom would be snapped up by a competitor long before a month was up. When she communicated this to Will, he told her he was terribly sorry, but she would have to follow the company's policies and procedures. She knew this would make them lose Tom. Not only would Capital View miss out on the opportunity to hire him, he might end up working for one of their direct competitors. And all of this was for no good reason other than Capital View's own antiquated polices. The whole situation made Maria extremely frustrated. This frustration had manifested itself into a craving for a hot dog with onions.

As she took that first, magnificent bite of her hot dog, Maria heard a familiar voice, "Gimme two with mustard, onions, and relish." So Will Peres was also a hot dog and onions person. At least there was one thing that they had in common.

He turned to her, looked at her hot dog, and smiled. "I'm glad to discover that you have at least one weakness."

She smiled back. "And it's nice to know it's one we share."

"Listen, I'm sorry about saying no to hiring Tom Washington. I know you're disappointed."

"It's not just disappointment about Tom. It's frustration about a system that is preventing me from doing exactly what I should be doing and what you hired me to do—bring top talent into the organization."

"Well, we have to follow established procedures."

"Why?"

"What do you mean 'why'?"

"Why do we have to follow established procedures?"

"Because they were established for a good reason."

"Can we at least revisit those reasons?"

"I'm not sure what that will accomplish." Will was getting a bit frustrated. He just wanted to enjoy his hot dogs.

Maria wasn't enjoying hers either. "At a minimum, it will help me understand the reasons for the procedures. And it might point out that the procedures aren't accomplishing their intended goals and need to be changed."

"I'm not going to get to enjoy my hot dogs unless I agree to this, am I?"

"Nope."

"Fine, then we can schedule a meeting. But before you ask, it can't be this afternoon."

"Why not?"

Will was laughing. "Because I don't think I can take you seriously with onions all over your blouse."

She was so embarrassed by the stain that she didn't bother to tell him he had relish in his teeth.

They met at 10 o'clock the following morning. Will had set aside an hour because he knew there was no such thing as a short conversation with Maria.

Will began, "Before you start, Maria, you should know that I'm not going to budge about changing our established procedures."

Wanna bet? Maria thought to herself. Out loud, she said, "Glad to hear you're keeping an open mind."

"Sorry, but we've had hiring procedures in place since long before you got here. They have served us well for a long time."

"Look, Will, you hired me to change the status quo around here. Can we at least discuss the procedures and see if they still make sense?"

"Sure, we can discuss them."

Small victories, Maria thought to herself, small victories.

"Let me start by asking when the hiring policies and procedures were first put into place?"

Will answered, "I don't know for sure, but they were in place when I was hired back in the mid-'80s."

"And what was the world of talent acquisition like back then?"

"I'm not sure I understand the question."

"What was the procedure when the company needed to hire someone? Walk me through the process."

Will chuckled. "It all started with an ad in the classified section of the newspaper. Remember help wanted ads?"

Maria laughed, "I barely remember newspapers!"

Will continued, "We would run an ad and usually get a boatload of responses in the mail." Will paused to think about the last time the company received a resume in the mail—he couldn't remember. "We would sift through the resumes, select the best five to 10, and invite people in for interviews."

"Then what?"

"Then we'd narrow the list down to the top three or four semi-finalists and invite them in for second interviews. We might interview the two finalists a third time, then we'd finally make our offer."

Maria recalled that process well. "Because the hiring process usually started with a help wanted ad, I guess it made sense that the position had budgetary approval before the process started."

"Sure."

"And because we had to wait for resumes to come in by mail and then invite people in for a few rounds of interviews, it made sense to ensure that a position was open for at least 10 business days before we made an offer."

"Absolutely."

And now Maria moved in for the kill. "Wouldn't you agree that the world has changed quite a bit since then?"

"Yes, but…"

"And doesn't it strike you as a bit unusual that our hiring policies have not changed since the days of newspaper ads and mailed in resumes?"

"OK, I get it." But Will wasn't ready to concede the point yet. "But these policies were instituted for other reasons."

"Go ahead."

"The need for budgetary approval and internal review before we post a position is an important fiscal safeguard. We can't just have managers hiring people willy-nilly without regard for financial consequences. You can understand that, can't you?"

"Absolutely," Maria agreed. "But I think we need to have the flexibility to make exceptions when we are presented with opportunities."

"But there are financial ramifications to these exceptions."

"Yes, but even assuming I make a generous offer to Tom, what percent of our payroll would that represent?"

"I get it. It would be less than 1 percent."

"It would be far less than 1 percent. For all intents and purposes, it would be a rounding error on our overall payroll."

"Still, we have budgets and payroll regulations for a reason."

"Absolutely. But I think we need the ability to occasionally make an exception to these regulations."

"What kind of exceptions?"

Maria said, "I'm a senior executive in this company and there is a wonderful opportunity to hire an exceptional executive with a proven track record. I'm not adding payroll willy-nilly—I'm making a strategic decision that will greatly benefit the company in the long run."

"But what if everyone in the company started doing things like this?"

Maria laughed, "I'm not sure it would be such a bad thing if everyone in the company were making strategic decisions that would benefit the company in the long run, but I know what you mean. I'm not saying everyone should have the power to hire someone whenever they feel like it. I'm saying that if we're serious about attracting top talent into this organization, we need to have the flexibility to bring people in without having an open requisition and waiting for the entire approval process. Senior executives should be able to make exceptions, or, if you're not comfortable with that, you should be able to make an exception if presented with a good business case by one of your executives."

"I get that, but Maria, you have to understand that there are also fairness issues at play here. One of the reasons we make sure that the position is posted for at least 10 business days is to ensure that people have an opportunity to apply for it. We might have internal people who want to apply for a job and we could pre-empt them if we just up and offer it to an outsider without a proper posting period."

"I get that, Will, I really do. But again, this is an exceptional case. It's a newly created, highly specialized position at a senior level that we just don't have the talent internally to fill. Tom Washington has done the job before and won awards for it. He's been on the cover of magazines! Just whom would we be acting unfairly toward if we hired Tom?"

"Well in this case, no one, but…"

"...but I'm not asking you to throw away our rules. I'm asking for the flexibility to make exceptions when we have a great opportunity. In this particular case, no one would be unfairly treated if we hire Tom, but the company would be hurt if we didn't hire him."

"Is this guy that important to you?"

"Yes, but that's not my point. What's most important to me is that Capital View has the ability to attract top talent into the organization."

"That's important to me, too."

"But now we have the opportunity to bring in top talent, and you're sitting there telling me I can't."

"I'm sorry, Maria, but my hands are tied."

"By who?"

"By our policies."

"And that's what I'm trying to get away from. Our company's policies aren't handed down by the federal government, Mount Olympus, or God Himself. We created these policies, and then we complain that we can't get around them. It's like tying our own hands and then complaining that our hands are tied. It's like shooting ourselves in the foot and then complaining that our foot hurts. It's like killing our parents and then complaining that we're orphans. It's like..."

"Calm down, Maria, I get it. Take a breath."

"Sorry, Will, I tend to get frustrated when something gets in the way of our ability to maximize the talent in our company. I realize that these rules may have been created for some good reasons. But over time, they might outlive their usefulness. In this case, I'm trying to bring talent into the company, and the rules are serving as what I call Talent Prevention Policies. Think of it this way, if you asked me, for some crazy reason, to come up a set of policies designed to prevent us from hiring a talented person when he becomes available, our current policies would probably be my exact plan. They would ensure that we couldn't make an offer to the guy for at least a month, and that would be enough time to ensure that he is no longer on the market."

"That is certainly not my intent or the intent of our rules."

"I know it's not the intent, but it is the result. Tom Washington is one of the most talented chief learning officers in the country and I want to bring him into our organization. And in this case, the only thing standing in the way is our own rules." She was very careful not to say that the only thing standing in the way was Will himself.

Will paused. He hadn't really thought of it that way. Policies and procedures were important. But so was attracting talent. Was it possible that the company's own policies and procedures were interfering with the company's ability to attract talent?

Will's tone became conciliatory. "OK, Maria, what are you suggesting?"

"Well," Maria wanted to be careful here, "putting the Tom Washington issue aside for a moment, we need to re-evaluate our policies. We need to make talent initiatives our top priority. Remember, people…"

"…are our most valuable asset," Will responded dutifully.

"Yes," Maria smiled, "and our best source of competitive advantage is having better people than our competitors. So we need to do whatever we can to continuously attract top talent into our organization. In some cases that might mean trying to recruit the best person into an opening. But in other cases, that might mean making an offer to talented people even when we don't have an opening. I think we all need to be talent scouts with our eyes open for talented people all the time."

"You're not suggesting that we expand our payroll every time we encounter someone who might be a good worker?"

"No, but I am suggesting that we be willing to bring someone into the organization whenever we encounter an exceptional talent."

"But the payroll ramifications…"

"…would be minimal. I'm not talking about good people. I'm talking about exceptional people. Research shows that top talent delivers anywhere from two to four times the value of the average, good employees. Therefore we need to do whatever we can to attract people like that into the organization and to keep them when we have them. Anything less and we're not really committed to having top talent in the organization."

"So we need to scrap our HR policies?" Will asked hesitantly. He wasn't sure he was ready to do that.

"No, we just need to be flexible within our policies. All I'm saying is that as a company and as senior executives, we need to make attracting top talent a priority.

And that means being flexible enough to do whatever it takes to bring in exceptional people, even if it means making exceptions to our rules. The idea is Talent Management Principle number three."

Talent Management Principle Number 3

Having better people is the best source of competitive advantage, so attracting top talent is a top priority. Be willing to do whatever it takes to bring in top talent. Do not let your own policies prevent you from hiring exceptional people.

"As usual, you're right, Maria." Will looked at his watch. "Our one-hour meeting has lasted almost two hours. Is that all?"

"Actually, there's one more thing. Can I hire Tom Washington?"

"Maria, at this point I'd let you hire George Washington if it would end this meeting. Yes, you can make him an offer. Now are we done?"

"Actually, there's one more thing…"

"Maria…" Will said threateningly.

"Don't worry. I just noticed it's almost noon. To thank you for your flexibility, I wanted to offer to buy the hot dogs today."

Will relaxed. "Maria, that's the best suggestion you've had yet."

Organizational Assessment

	NOT AT ALL		NEUTRAL		TO A GREAT EXTENT
1. Does your organization state that attracting top talent is a priority?	1	2	3	4	5
2. Does your organization behave as if attracting top talent really is a priority?	1	2	3	4	5
3. Does your organization avoid the practice of having talent acquisition policies that were designed for a world other than the world that we live in?	1	2	3	4	5
4. Does your organization avoid the practice of having policies in areas other than talent acquisition that seem to accomplish the exact opposite of their original intent?	1	2	3	4	5
5. Does your organization have the flexibility and agility to make exceptions to rules and policies when they run counter to the organization's best interests?	1	2	3	4	5
6. Does your organization encourage people at all levels and in all functions to be talent scouts who are constantly on the lookout for top talent?	1	2	3	4	5
7. To what extent is your organization able to attract top talent?	1	2	3	4	5

Questions for Personal Reflection

1. Was there anything described in chapter 3 that seemed descriptive of your organization?

2. What can you do if you see what Maria calls a Talent Prevention Policy in your organization?

3. What can you do if you see a policy that was designed for a good reason, but in a world very different from the one we live in today?

4. What can you do to ensure that your organization's policies and procedures are aligned with their intent?

5. What can you do to be a talent scout who is constantly on the lookout for top talent? What can you do to encourage others to be talent scouts?

6. What can you do to help attract top talent into your organization?

7. What can you do to ensure that attracting top talent is really a priority?

D ammit, we just lost another one!"

Everyone turned and looked at Dave Marx, the chief technology officer. The executive team was in its weekly meeting and Regina Clark, the chief marketing officer, was reporting on marketing initiatives. Dave, as always, had one eye on his smartphone and interrupted the meeting with his sudden outcry.

Will turned to him, "Dave, are you checking out the Mets again?"

"No, Will. I've just lost another manager from an important position. Alan Saffran just gave his notice."

"Do you know why?"

"No, but I intend to find out. I'm really surprised about Alan. He's always seemed happy here and we just promoted him to manager six months ago. This is the third manager I've lost in the last three months. It's starting to feel like an epidemic."

Will appeared concerned. "Do we know why the other two left?"

"They both said, 'It just wasn't a good fit.'"

"That's funny," Regina chimed in.

"How is that funny?" Dave asked, annoyed.

"One of my managers gave notice last week and said the same thing."

Maria decided it was time to join the conversation. "This actually is starting to sound like an epidemic. We've lost four managers in the last month?"

Now it was Bobby's turn. "Actually, it's six. I've lost a couple as well."

"And we don't know why?" Maria asked.

Everyone was silent. Maria continued, "Does anyone mind if I review the exit interview data? I'd also like to do some digging and see if I can find out what's really going on."

Will said, "I think that's a great idea. We really can't afford to be losing talent."

He was concerned about his chief technology officer. Dave Marx had the reputation of being one of the best tech guys on Wall Street, but perhaps his skills as a manager were lacking. Will feared that Dave might be driving away good talent. But he wasn't the only one, Regina and Bobby were losing good people too. He hoped Maria would get some answers quickly.

Will didn't have to wait very long. Maria asked for a little time on the agenda of the following week's executive team meeting.

She wasted little time in getting started. "I think I've figured out why we're losing managers," she said.

Will asked, "Were you able to find something in the exit interviews?"

"Not really." Maria had discovered that exit interviews were conducted on employees' last day at the company. They were eager to get out of there and typically just gave perfunctory answers. That's why the exit interview data typically showed a lot of "it just wasn't a good fit" types of responses without any depth or context. In her experience, the best way to get good exit interview data was to do the interview a few weeks after the employee left and have it conducted by a third party.

"So how did you reach your conclusions?"

"I tracked down the dearly departed and had some conversations with them."

"I'm almost afraid to ask." Will said. He knew that the number one reason why people leave organizations is because of their manager.

It was almost as if Maria had read his mind. "Don't worry everybody. I spoke to six recent departures, and none of them said they didn't like their bosses. As a matter of fact, I heard nothing but respect for the executives in this room. And they loved the company and appreciated the opportunities they were given."

Dave was frustrated. "If they like the bosses and like the company, then why on earth would they leave? We pay them enough!"

Maria continued, "It wasn't the money either. It was the work."

Will leaned forward. "What about the work?"

"I had a long talk with Alan Saffran. Alan loved software engineering. It was all he ever wanted to do since high school."

Dave jumped in, "And he was great at it. The best I ever saw. He was so good that I really believed he earned a promotion. As soon as there was an opening, I promoted him to be the manager of the department."

"And that was the problem," Maria said. She let this sink in for a moment.

Dave looked confused. "How could that be a problem? I gave him a promotion and a big raise."

"Yes, but you took him out of a role he loved and put him into a job he didn't really want to do and was ill-suited for. He gave notice because he's been unhappy. He took a job at another company that was going to let him do software engineering without having to manage people."

Regina joined in. "Uh oh."

Will turned to her. "What's the matter, Regina?"

"I think I did the same thing. I felt that one of our top salespeople, Stephanie Reid, had earned a promotion last year. I took her out of the field and made her a sales manager. She quit last month."

Maria nodded. "I talked to Stephanie. She loved sales and she loved being out in the field talking to customers. She didn't love being cooped up in headquarters spending most of her time in meetings."

Will was beginning to understand. "Are you saying that we're 'rewarding' our best employees by promoting them into roles they don't want to be in, and that's why we're losing them?"

Maria smiled. "I used to think this was the problem."

Now Will was confused. "And now you don't think it's a problem?"

Maria smiled. "No. Now I'm convinced it's two problems. The first is that we're creating managers who don't really want to be managers and aren't very good at it. The bigger problem is that we're removing our best engineers and salespeople."

Will looked troubled. "Isn't it traditional to promote your best employees?"

"Yes, it's traditional. But it's dead wrong. Let's look at the two mistakes one at a time. First, there's the problem of the promotion to a managerial role. The job of manager is a hard one. The textbooks tell us that at a fundamental level, it involves planning, organizing, leading, and controlling. These are difficult skills to master. Beyond that, the job involves technical skills and people skills. We've already agreed that the most important job of a manager is hiring, developing, engaging, and retaining good people. Managing people is a delicate operation and not everyone is suited for it. We promote the people with the best technical skills. These people are sometimes not the ones with the best people management skills. Sometimes we're moving them from a job they're great at to one they're not so good at. Even worse, we frequently don't give them any guidance or training. And sometimes this means we're moving them from a job they love to one they don't enjoy. And that's why we lose them."

Will had to admit this made sense. "And what about the second problem?"

Maria went on, "This one might be even worse. We're removing our most talented performers from important roles. Take Stephanie—she was a great salesperson. When we took her out of the field, we replaced her with someone less experienced and less skilled. We need great salespeople in the field."

Regina interrupted, "Yes, but Stephanie was also a pretty good manager."

"Sure," Maria agreed. "But we took a great salesperson and turned her into a pretty good manager. Which do you think is more valuable to our organization?"

Dave Marx asked, "So what do we do?" He knew he had done the same thing with Alan Saffran. He had turned a great software engineer into a pretty good manager. Moreover, he realized that he had turned a happy engineer into an unhappy manager. Finally, he had turned a productive employee into an ex-employee.

"I'll tell you what we do," Maria said emphatically. "We stop doing it."

Will saw another problem, "But if we don't promote our best employees, won't they feel underappreciated? And won't they leave anyway?"

Maria understood the problem. "We really do need to show our most talented employees that we appreciate them. We need to reward them for their good work. But these rewards need to be in ways other than promotion. We need to separate rewards from promotions."

"But aren't promotions seen as the best rewards?"

"That's how they've been seen traditionally, but in many cases it's been dead wrong. That's not how Stephanie wanted to be rewarded. That's not how Alan wanted to be rewarded."

"I see where you're going with this," Will said. "How should we reward our most talented people?"

"It depends," Maria answered. "Stephanie was a salesperson. She liked to see her successes rewarded monetarily. She liked bonuses and commissions. Money is also how many salespeople keep score. The promotion and the new title were not really important for her. Alan was different. For him, it was all about the work. He liked challenging work, and the way we could have rewarded and motivated him was by coming up with new challenges."

"So whom do we promote? If we don't promote our best people, then how do we fill our managerial jobs?"

Bobby chimed in. "I guess I do things a little differently," he said. "I don't automatically promote the best performers."

Will was curious. "How do you do it Bobby?" he asked.

"I tend to reward loyalty. I had an opening for an accounting manager last month. We have some young hotshot accountants who are pretty good. But I felt they haven't paid their dues. Walt Williams had been in that department for 16 years. I felt his seniority should be rewarded, so I gave him the manager job."

Maria jumped in. "Has Walt demonstrated skills in planning, organizing, leading, and controlling?"

"He's an accountant—he's great at the controlling part of the job."

Maria ignored the laughter and continued, "Does he have great people management skills?"

"Well, he's OK at it, I guess. I just felt his seniority and loyalty should be rewarded."

Maria was getting excited, "I get that, but our managerial jobs are too important to be given to anyone other than the best person for the job. Bobby, would you ever hire an accountant who had no training or experience in accounting?"

"Of course not."

"Dave, would you ever hire a software engineer who had no training or experience in engineering?"

"Of course not."

"Would we ever hire a manager who has no training or experience in management? From what I'm hearing, we do it all the time!"

Will wanted to calm her down. "So Maria, let me ask you again," he said slowly. "Who do we promote? If it's not our top performers or our most senior people, how do we fill our managerial jobs?"

"This may sound obvious, but it needs to be said. We should fill our managerial jobs with people who possess the skills to do the managerial jobs. In some cases it may be the top performers or the senior people, but we need to look at their skills. The skills needed for the individual contributor jobs are very different from the skills needed for managerial jobs. Frequently, the person with the best skills for the managerial job will not be the best performers in the individual contributor job. But we need to promote the person who would be best suited for the next job, not the person who performed best in the previous job, and certainly not the person who had lasted longest in the previous job without ever getting promoted."

"This all makes sense, but I see a problem," Will said; sometimes he thought his greatest skill was in seeing potential problems. "Won't the top performers start to feel resentful if we promote lesser performers over them?"

Maria answered immediately, "Not if we reward them appropriately."

"I see a couple of potential problems with that." Will was at it again. "First, might that mean that in some cases, an employee might make more money than his manager?"

"Sure, what's the problem?"

Will had to think about that one. "It's not commonly done."

"Sure it is. In professional sports, the star athletes always make more money than their coaches."

"I can see it in sports. People go to the games to see the stars, not the coaches."

"Why?"

"Because the stars contribute more to winning than the coaches."

"Isn't that true here as well? Don't our star performers contribute more to the success of the company than the best managers?"

Will conceded the point. "You're right. It's a bit unusual, but I guess I could wrap my head around an employee making more money than his manager—provided the employee was a top performer."

Maria wasn't done. "But it won't always be about money. Sometimes the top performers want to be rewarded in other ways. We have plenty of ways to reward employees: challenging work assignments, flexible hours, work from home opportunities…"

"That was the second problem I saw. How do we know which employees want to be managers and how do we know how to reward the others?"

"That one's simple, Will. We talk to them."

"Maria, you and I don't have time to talk to every employee in our company and find out what they want."

"No, that's why we have managers. Over the past week, I've taken the time to talk to employees who have recently given notice."

"And we got some good information from those interviews."

"Yes, but think of it this way: In addition to conducting exit interviews, why don't we have our managers conduct stay interviews?"

"Stay interviews?"

"Yes, they're just like exit interviews, but conducted with current employees and in the present tense instead of the past tense. Instead of asking ex-employees what they liked and didn't like and why they left, we should ask current employees what they like and don't like, what might make them want to stay and what might make them want to leave."

"Wouldn't that be time-consuming for our managers?"

"Yes, but it's a lot less time-consuming than hiring and training replacements. Think of it this way: have you ever gone to a doctor when you were healthy, just to get a check-up?"

"Sure."

"A stay interview is a check-up. An exit interview is an autopsy. We're trying to find out what killed the patient, but he's already gone. Just as a check-up might prevent an autopsy, a stay interview might save us from having to do an exit interview."

Maria turned to Dave. "Dave, do you realize that if we knew six months ago that Alan didn't want to be a manager and just wanted more challenging work, that he might have never given notice?"

Dave answered, "Possibly, but if he didn't want to be a manager, why did he accept the promotion in the first place?"

"Two reasons. I asked around and discovered that around here, if you don't accept new assignments when asked, you're viewed as not being a team player and as lacking ambition. Also, you threw a boatload of money at him. That's hard to turn down."

It was Regina's turn. "Maria, don't even ask," she said. "I'm sure I could have saved Stephanie's career with Capital View if I had only asked her what she wanted."

Will tried to move the conversation to looking forward, not backward. "So what exactly are you suggesting here, Maria?"

"First of all, we need to talk to our people. We need to find out which ones really want a career in management. A lot of people start out wanting to climb the corporate ladder. Some discover that managing people is no fun and they don't really like it. They continue doing it because that's how a career is supposed to progress and that's where the money is. For those who don't really want to spend their careers doing management stuff, we should be able to create a career path in which they can do what they love, contribute to the company, and be rewarded appropriately. For the people who really want to be in management, we should identify them and try to build their skills appropriately so that they can have a career doing what they want to do, while also contributing to the company and being rewarded appropriately. And by having these conversations, hopefully we can also find out who's happy and who's unhappy. This will probably help our turnover problem."

"It sounds like a lot of work—having in-depth conversation with all of our employees about their desires and skills."

"It is. That's why a lot of people don't want to be managers!" Everyone laughed. "But the job of the manager is to keep employees engaged, productive, and employed at this company. Good managers know that the best way to do this is to keep employees challenged and give them work they enjoy and are good at it. This is where the skill of the manager comes in and this is how they add value."

"And?" Will said, he knew there was more.

"And we need to change how we fill our manager jobs. Promoting based on past performance or seniority won't cut it."

"After hearing you describe this problem—excuse me—two problems, I'm kind of embarrassed that we've been doing things this way for so long."

"Don't be embarrassed. In my experience, most organizations have always done things that way. It's so prevalent that it's led to one of my Talent Management Principles."

Talent Management Principle Number 4
The job of manager requires specific skills and abilities. Promotion should be based on the ability to do the next job, not performance in the current job. Good performance should be rewarded appropriately, but promotion should not be a reward for past performance.

Will listened attentively. "Thanks, Maria, I think this has been helpful for all of us."

Dave suddenly interrupted shouting, "Dammit, we just lost another one!"

Will had to ask, "Did we really just lose another manager?"

"No, the Mets just lost again."

Organizational Assessment

	NOT AT ALL		NEUTRAL		TO A GREAT EXTENT
1. To what extent does your organization get good information from exit interviews?	1	2	3	4	5
2. Does your organization use the information from its exit interviews?	1	2	3	4	5
3. Do you know the reasons why people leave your organization?	1	2	3	4	5
4. Does your organization avoid the practice of promoting people into new roles based on their performance in previous roles?	1	2	3	4	5
5. Does your organization avoid the practice of promoting people based on seniority?	1	2	3	4	5
6. Does your organization avoid the practice of promoting people into roles that they are not suited for?	1	2	3	4	5
7. Does your organization avoid the practice of moving people out of roles they are good at and enjoy?	1	2	3	4	5
8. When your organization puts people into managerial roles, does it give them the training and skills they need to succeed?	1	2	3	4	5
9. Do you reward your people for good performance in ways other than promotions?	1	2	3	4	5
10. Do you place people into managerial roles by assessing the match between their skills and managerial competencies?	1	2	3	4	5
11. Does your organization have a path that enables top performers to advance in status and compensation without becoming managers of people?	1	2	3	4	5

Questions for Personal Reflection

1. Was there anything described in chapter 4 that seemed descriptive of your organization?

2. Would your organization benefit from conducting stay interviews? Do you believe you would conduct fewer exit interviews if you did stay interviews?

3. What can you do to help prevent perpetuating the cycle of promoting based on past performance in a different role?

4. What can you do to help ensure that people are deployed in roles they are best suited for, enjoy, and are likely to remain in?

5. What can you do to ensure that managerial positions are filled by people with the right skills?

5

I 've got some good news and some bad news."

Karen Michaels, the COO, approached Maria in the break room. Maria thought, *at least the glass is half full. For once Karen isn't coming to me just with a problem.*

"OK, Karen, what's the good news?" Maria asked.

"The good news is that we're doing much better at putting the right people into supervisory positions."

It had been six months since they had talked about actually looking at managerial aptitude for supervisory positions instead of promoting based on individual contributor performance. Karen seemed proud of her division's newfound ability to put the right people into manager positions.

"Sounds great," Maria said. "Can I leave now before the other shoe drops?"

"No such luck. The bad news is that my managers—the veterans as well as the new ones—are not embracing the new mindset that managers are not just responsible for making their numbers, but that they also need to take responsibility for hiring, developing, engaging, and retaining their people."

Maria had been about to pour herself a decaf, but after hearing this, she went for the high octane. She knew she was going to have her work cut out for her on this one.

When she had accepted the job, Will had charged Maria with creating a talent mindset and having that mindset permeate throughout the company. Maria remembered when the topic first came up—it was her first executive team meeting. At that meeting, the executive team realized that managers were not doing an especially good job of focusing on the talent management part of the job. Maria was proud that she had gotten the rest of the executive team—especially Karen—to agree that managers should be focusing on hiring, developing, engaging, and retaining talented people. Karen had bought into the mindset, but it sounded like she was having some trouble with the execution.

"What seems to be the problem?"

"Well, I had informed all of my managers about the new mindset and the new expectations. They all said they understood the idea that they should be focusing on talent and they agreed that they would spend more time working on talent issues."

"So what happened?"

"It's been six months, and I just got the numbers. Our turnover is right where it always was and our engagement scores have actually gone down a bit."

Maria was gratified that Karen was looking at engagement and turnover numbers instead of just focusing on financial metrics. The finances were vitally important, but engagement and retention tend to be excellent leading indicators of future financial performance.

While Karen's new focus on nonfinancial metrics was a step in the right direction, the problem she was describing was anything but. "Can you pinpoint any reasons why the new initiatives aren't working?"

"Actually, that's what I was hoping you could do for me."

"Well, I can't answer the question right now, but I can work with you to see how we might find some answers."

"OK, where do we begin?"

"I'd like to start by talking to your managers, preferably one-by-one. Do you have any meetings scheduled?"

"Actually, the timing is perfect. I'll be conducting my annual performance reviews with my managers starting on Monday."

"Mind if I sit in?"

"Not at all. I'm up for anything that might help us figure this out and drive better results."

They agreed to get started on Monday morning with the first of the annual performance reviews.

The first meeting on Monday was with Laurie Kelly. Laurie was one of the most senior managers in the company. She was well-respected by senior management and had a reputation for being an excellent manager who always delivered good results.

Laurie walked into Karen's office and the first thing she said was, "What's she doing here?" She was referring to Maria.

Maria thought, people see someone from HR and assume there's trouble.

Karen laughed and said, "Nothing to worry about, Laurie. I asked Maria to sit in to help me be a better manager of managers."

"So I'm not getting fired?"

Maria knew that was the first thing people thought when they someone from HR sitting in on a meeting with their manager.

"No," Karen said "Not today," she added with a laugh.

"And I'm not in trouble?"

Boy, HR really does have a bad reputation, Maria thought. In fairness, it might be well-deserved.

"No trouble at all." Karen said, then got down to business, "Let's begin your annual performance review."

Karen had been well-trained on performance reviews. She knew to start with the positives. She started with the company's favorite statistic: billable hours. "Laurie, I see that your department exceeded its goal for billable hours last year."

"Yes, thank you," she said. "We all worked very hard."

"And I see that your department's profitability also exceeded goal."

"Yes we did. We're happy to contribute."

Maria watched as Karen and Laurie spent about 10 minutes discussing billable hours and profitability. She knew that Laurie and her group worked hard and thought it was a bit odd that an entire year's performance was discussed in one meeting a year. She made a mental note to work on having performance discussions happen more frequently.

After about 10 minutes, the conversation shifted. Karen said, "OK, Laurie, now let's discuss your development opportunities."

In performance reviews, there were no negatives. There were just positives and "development opportunities." Maria also thought it was a bit odd that not only did the performance conversations happen only once a year, but the areas of excellent performance only took up about 10 minutes of the hour-long meeting. Laurie was, by all accounts, a very good employee, and her contributions to the company were only acknowledged for about 10 minutes a year. *I guess we need the rest of the hour to fix her weaknesses,* Maria thought sadly. She was making a lot of mental notes.

Karen made her transition. "Laurie, while you had a great year, there are a couple of areas that I'd like you to work on. Remember when we discussed focusing on hiring, developing, engaging, and retaining employees?"

"Sure," Laurie said.

"Well I noticed that your department's engagement scores were below the target we had set and actually below the company average," Karen said.

"Uh huh," Laurie acknowledged.

"I'd like to see those come up for next year."

"OK."

"And your turnover remains high—nearly 20 percent last year."

"Yeah."

"That has to come down."

"OK."

"And I noticed in the area of development, your department hardly ever utilizes our training and development opportunities."

"I guess."

"Can you explain this?"

"I guess it's because I've got good people and they don't really need much in the way of training and development."

Karen nodded. "Fair enough," She said. "But even the best employees can improve. I think your department needs to do a better job of taking advantage of the opportunities that the company offers."

Laurie shrugged. "We'll try. But remember, time my consultants spend in class is not billable," she said. "If we do more training, we'll have fewer billable hours and you just complimented me on my department's numbers in that area."

"OK, but let's see if we can do better in engagement, retention, and training next year, OK?"

"Sure."

"I'll write those down as your goals for improvement for this year."

"OK."

"Is there anything you'd like to add?"

"Not really." Laurie had been pretty animated during the discussions about billable hours and profitability. Maria couldn't help but notice that the discussion of talent management issues resulted in mostly monosyllabic answers from Laurie.

Laurie looked a bit impatient. "Can we discuss my bonus?" She said.

"Sure." Karen pulled out the calculations. Managers were incentivized based on billable hours and profitability, so Laurie was due quite a large bonus. Naturally, she was pretty animated once again during the discussion of her bonus money.

The meeting wound down. It turned out they didn't even need a full hour to discuss Laurie's performance over the past year. Laurie thanked Karen, but still eyed Maria suspiciously as she left.

"So, how'd I do?" Karen asked Maria.

"You did fine," Maria acknowledged, as Karen smiled, "given the limitations of our system."

Uh oh, thought Karen, I couldn't get away with just a compliment. Out loud, she said, "The limitations of our system?"

"Did you notice that Laurie was more than happy to discuss billable hours and profitability, but she pretty much shut down when you brought up engagement, retention, and training."

"Sure," Karen said. "I figured that like most people, she was just more comfortable discussing her successes than the areas that need improvement."

"Maybe, but I think it's more than that."

Karen had a few more ideas. "You've got to understand, Maria, that we've been discussing billable hours and profitability around here for years. The talent management initiatives are pretty new. I only brought them to Laurie's attention about six months ago, so she's probably not as comfortable with her role as a talent manager as she is about managing the other areas. She'll come around."

"I don't think so."

"Why not? You heard her agree to do a better job in these areas."

"I heard her say she'll try. I heard her say, 'OK' when you told her those would be goals for the upcoming year. But I didn't hear any real conviction or commitment."

"And I suppose you've got an explanation for this?"

"As a matter of fact I do." Karen settled back in her chair as Maria started talking. "First of all, like most managers, Laurie is smart. She knows what the incentives are and she knows how to achieve them. When we incentivize her to meet specific goals in billable hours and profitability, that's what she's going to focus on. We can talk about training and development all we want, but if she's going to get paid on billable hours, that's what she's going to focus on. Moreover, she might view the other initiatives as being counterproductive to the incentivized goals. Time spent on the other incentives might take away from her ability to achieve the primary goals."

"I get that."

"During the meeting, Laurie was only interested in discussing areas that contributed to her bonus. She was restless during the rest of the conversation because she didn't think those things mattered."

Karen became a bit defensive. "That's not entirely true," she said. "I met with her six months ago and told her about the new initiatives and how important they were. I know she understood and she agreed to work on those areas."

"I'm sure she did," Maria replied. "But even though you brought these issues up in her performance review, there were no incentives or consequences. All of the incentives were around billable hours and profitability, so that's what she was focused on."

"Yes, but don't forget, billable hours and profitability are the engines that drive this company."

"Absolutely," Maria agreed. "But by single-mindedly focusing on achieving short-term results in these areas, we lose focus on future growth and profitability opportunities. While her department's performance this year was admirable, I think the engagement and turnover numbers predict lower productivity for the upcoming year. Laurie gets paid based on certain billable hours and profitability goals for a single year. Therefore, she will focus on these goals without looking ahead at longer term goals or bigger picture issues."

Karen felt compelled to defend her employee, "So are you suggesting that Laurie doesn't care about the company and is only interested in money?"

"No, Karen," Maria said. "I'm suggesting that Laurie is behaving perfectly rationally. Throughout the course of a year, we give our managers lots of goals and initiatives. But when we tie bonuses and incentives to certain goals, we are sending the message that those are the most important. I wouldn't expect Laurie to do anything other than focus on the goals with bonuses and pay less attention to the other initiatives. This isn't her fault, it's ours."

Karen noted that Maria included herself in the blame and wasn't just pointing fingers at Karen. "Did you notice anything else?"

"Well, yes. You did bring up engagement, retention, and employee development at the end of the meeting…"

"I know. I told her those would be goals for next year, but I failed to attach any rewards or incentives."

"Yes, that's part of it," Maria said. "But you also didn't give her any specific goals in those areas. The discussion was about a general need to improve. Her turnover is about 20 percent. If she gets it to 19 percent next year, she can cite improvement, even though that result is not really what we would like to see."

"Good point. So what do we do?"

"We need to recognize that our managers are smart, rational people and they will pursue the rewards we offer them. When we choose to reward certain areas, we send the message that these are most important. Initiatives without rewards are perceived as being less of a priority, no matter how much we tell people that they are important. So if we want our managers to pursue a certain course of action, we need to hold them accountable. There should be specific, measurable goals, not vague generalizations. And if we really want them to achieve those goals, we need to hold them accountable. We can't just expect them to focus on certain initiatives while we are busy rewarding other behaviors."

"That makes sense," Karen conceded. "We've been throwing a lot of initiatives at our managers over the years, but not really holding them accountable."

"The lack of accountability is a problem in a lot of organizations. It's especially relevant to managers and it ties in pretty well why so many organizations tell managers how important the talent management functions are, but so few managers really execute in this area—it's the lack of accountability. We all agreed as an executive team that this is an important priority for our managers and we communicated it to our managers, but we didn't follow through by holding them accountable. It's something we've known for a long time, but so many of us ignore it that's it's one of my Talent Management Principles."

> ## Talent Management Principle Number 5
> Employees are smart and know how to pursue rewards. If you want to see certain behaviors and results, hold employees accountable. It's irrational to expect employees to deliver outcomes if we do not hold them accountable.

"This makes sense," Karen said, "but I have a bit of a problem with this."

"What's that?" asked Maria.

"Why didn't you tell me this principle before I conducted my performance review with Laurie?"

"Good point. At least we'll be able to do better with the rest of the reviews you've got scheduled. And maybe we can call Laurie back in and offer her some incentives and accountabilities. And while we're at it, perhaps we can review performance more frequently than at one year intervals."

Fortunately for Maria, they agreed to meet with their managers twice a year. Unfortunately, it would be another six months before Karen and Maria discovered another hole in their plan.

Organizational Assessment

	NOT AT ALL		NEUTRAL		TO A GREAT EXTENT
1. Does your organization have performance review conversations more frequently than once a year?	1	2	3	4	5
2. Does your organization's performance review focus more on positives and the development of strengths than on negatives and the fixing of weaknesses?	1	2	3	4	5
3. Does your organization avoid the practice of giving managers numerous initiatives and priorities, but only holding them accountable for a few?	1	2	3	4	5
4. Does your organization give specific, measurable goals to managers and employees?	1	2	3	4	5
5. Does your organization hold its employees and managers accountable for doing the things you ask of them and delivering expected results?	1	2	3	4	5
6. Do people in your organization view human resources personnel as being helpful and valuable (as opposed to only showing up when someone is in trouble)?	1	2	3	4	5

Questions for Personal Reflection

1. Was there anything described in chapter 5 that seemed descriptive of your organization?

2. What can you do to ensure that people's performance is reviewed more frequently than once a year?

3. What can you do to ensure that performance reviews focus more on positives and the development of strengths than on negatives and the fixing of weaknesses?

4. What can you do to give employees goals that are more specific and measurable?

5. What can you do to ensure that employees are held accountable for doing what is asked of them and delivering expected results?

K aren had finally followed some of Maria's advice. She had agreed to do performance reviews twice a year instead of once. Six months after Maria sat in on Laurie Kelly's review, the three of them sat down for another review.

"I see you've invited her again." Laurie spoke to Karen about Maria, but didn't address Maria.

Maria chose to respond. "I hope you don't mind," she said neutrally.

"Let's get on with it." Laurie said. She didn't seem to be dripping with enthusiasm about the review. Previously, the annual reviews ended with a bonus discussion. Now that they were doing semi-annual reviews, today's meeting wouldn't result in a bonus for Laurie. Maria couldn't help but notice that she didn't seem as interested in a review that merely discussed her performance.

Karen dove right in. "I apologize," she said. "But I haven't had a chance to check out the numbers before today's meeting. Let's review the numbers together."

"OK," Laurie said, a bit hesitantly. Maria got the impression that Laurie had checked out the numbers and knew what was coming.

Karen was frowning. "Let's start with billable hours," Karen said. "Your mid-year numbers are way down from last year. As a matter of fact," Karen paused for a moment to check her calculator, "you're running a bit behind the pace to meet your target for the year." Karen stopped to give Laurie a chance to respond.

"Yeah," was all Laurie offered.

"OK, let's take a look at profit. It looks like your profit numbers are also down from last year."

"Yes, it's been a tough couple of quarters."

"Any idea why your numbers are down?"

"Not really. My people seem to be working just as hard as ever," Laurie said a bit defensively.

Karen seemed puzzled. "So if your people are working just as hard, why would billable hours be down?"

"I guess it's because we've been a bit shorthanded. But don't worry, I've just hired a new batch of consultants, so our hours should be coming up very soon."

Karen seemed satisfied, "Let's move on."

Maria wasn't satisfied. "May I interject something here?"

"Sure," Karen said.

"Of course," Laurie said, but her body language begged to differ.

"I think we need to figure out why the numbers are down," said Maria.

"We've just covered that," Laurie said with a hint of hostility. "We've been shorthanded."

"I understand," Maria said. "But I think we need to look at why you've been shorthanded."

"The answer is simple enough," Laurie said impatiently. "We've had a lot of consultants quit."

"Yes, but I think we need to look at why they quit."

"They found other jobs. The economy's been improving, so there are more jobs out there and good people have more options."

"Yes, but we need to look at why they were looking for other jobs and why they selected other options rather than continuing to work here." Maria was employing a technique called the Five Levels of Why. You keep asking why until you get down to the root cause of a problem.

Laurie looked like she was about to boil over, but before she could respond, Karen intervened. "What are you getting at, Maria?" she asked.

"When we met six months ago, we noticed pretty high turnover rate in Laurie's department. We also noticed below-average engagement scores."

"Yes, but my billable hours and profitability were just fine," Laurie said. "They were better than fine—they were ahead of my goals." Laurie figured the best defense was a good offense.

"Yes, but the billable hours and profitability numbers were looking back at the previous year," Maria said. "Turnover and engagement scores are good leading indicators of future performance. I was concerned back then that the poor turnover and engagement numbers were going to translate into some challenges for the upcoming year, and that's what we're seeing now. That's why focusing exclusively on short-term measurements—even if they are the important measures for our organization—doesn't always translate to long-term success. "

Karen said, "Yes, and that's why we made talent management part of Laurie's plan for the year."

Sure enough, after the previous review, Karen had included improved retention, employee engagement, and effective hiring as part of Laurie's responsibilities and accountabilities for the current year.

"Yes," said Laurie, looking a bit relieved. "Why don't we look at some of those numbers?"

"OK," Karen started turning pages in her binder. "It looks like your turnover for the first half of the year is running at 18 percent. That doesn't sound so good," Karen said mildly, trying not to be too confrontational.

"Actually," Laurie said, "it's an improvement. I was at 20 percent last year, so we're looking at a 10 percent improvement in turnover."

Maria was concerned about the high turnover number and feared that beyond the high number, there were probably some very talented consultants leaving the organization. But Karen let this pass.

"Let's see what we've got in engagement. In our most recent engagement survey, your department was at 65 percent."

"Yes. That's up from the last survey when we were at 62 percent."

Maria was now very concerned. Companywide, the percentage of employees who fell into the categories of "engaged" or "highly engaged" was 79 percent. Laurie was bragging about being at 65 percent. Laurie also seemed content with an 18 percent turnover number. Even more troubling, Karen seemed to be letting Laurie slide with these numbers. Maria decided to let Karen continue with the review before stepping in.

"Finally, let's look at hiring. How are you doing in this area, Laurie?"

"We're doing great," Laurie said. "Over 90 percent of my new hires have MBAs from top-10 schools. More than half have more than two years of consulting experience. I think I've done an excellent job of bringing in new talent."

"Excellent," said Karen.

Not necessarily excellent, thought Maria.

After the down numbers in billable hours and profitability, Karen thought it would be a good idea to offer some compliments. "Laurie, I'm glad we made the talent management functions part of your accountabilities," she said. "It sounds like you're doing a good job of improving retention and engagement and that you've really stepped up your hiring."

"I'm sorry, but I feel like I've got to intervene here," Maria said. "I don't think we should be celebrating 18 percent turnover or engagement scores that are 14 points below the company average."

"Wait a minute," Laurie said angrily. "My boss told me that part of my accountability for the year was to improve retention and engagement. I've shown improvement in both."

Maria turned to Karen. "What were the targets for retention and engagement in Laurie's plan?"

Karen pulled out the paperwork. "It looks like we wrote in, 'Employee's department will demonstrate improved retention. Employee's department will demonstrate an increase in engagement scores as measured by the company's semi-annual engagement survey.' That's what we had agreed upon."

"So there were no specific targets or measurable goals?"

Karen was a bit embarrassed. "I guess not," she said.

"Look, you told me to improve and I improved," Laurie said, rising to her own defense. "End of story."

Not end of story, thought Maria, not by a longshot.

"What about hiring?" asked Maria.

"What about it?" asked Karen in response.

"What were Laurie's goals regarding improvements in hiring?"

"Let's see. We wrote, 'Employee will demonstrate improvement in the area of talent acquisition.'"

"That's it?" Maria asked.

"What do you mean, 'That's it?'" Karen said. "You encouraged us to start holding our managers more accountable for talent management practices, so I built more effective hiring right into her annual performance goals." Now it was Karen's turn to be defensive.

"Yes, but you didn't include any description of what 'improvement in the area of talent acquisition really means.' How will we measure it?" asked Maria.

"I can answer that," Laurie said. "I've been hiring MBAs from top-10 schools. I've also been hiring more experienced consultants."

"Also," Karen said, jumping in. "I've been looking at some other hiring metrics. Laurie's been filling her positions relatively quickly and at a pretty reasonable cost. I know HR people like to look at those measures as well." She looked at Maria hopefully, but Maria was just shaking her head.

"I don't care about any of that stuff."

"What do you care about?" Karen asked, a bit frustrated.

"I care about whether the person we've hired performs well on the job. You can hire tons of people quickly and cheaply, but if they don't perform well, it's not a good hire."

"But I've hired good people," Laurie added. "Just look at their credentials."

"I did," Maria said. "I noticed you hired one consultant who graduated near the top of her class at Harvard Business School."

"Yes, she also had financial consulting experience."

"And I noticed she quit after three months," Maria said. "She might have looked like a great hire on paper, but if she quit after three months, she didn't contribute to our company's success. And given the time and money invested in hiring her and the fact that we then had to start the hiring process again, hiring her cost us money. No matter how impressive her credentials were, this was not a good hire."

"OK, Maria, what's your point?" asked Karen.

"I'm saying that we can't judge the quality of a hire based on credentials, time to fill, or cost. The only way we can really know if a new hire is any good is based on performance on the job."

"But it takes a long time before a person settles into a job, learns the ropes, and starts performing." Karen said.

"Absolutely," Maria replied. "So we really can't judge the quality of a hire for at least six months after the person starts. And it probably makes more sense to wait at least a year, if not longer."

"So are you saying Laurie didn't do a good job of hiring this year?"

"Not at all. I'm saying we won't know how good of a job she did in hiring this year until next year. We need to see if her new hires remain on the job and perform well."

"Fair enough," Karen agreed. "So we'll pick this up next year. Laurie's off the hook for now."

"OK." Maria paused briefly before adding, "But we're not off the hook. The problem wasn't that we might have looked at the wrong metrics for hiring. The problem is that we didn't include any metrics in Laurie's plan."

Karen said, "I don't understand. You convinced me that we should be holding our managers accountable for talent management practices. So I included retention, engagement, and hiring in Laurie's plan."

"Yes, but there were no measures included. Accountability without measurement doesn't work."

"I think I'm starting to see the problem," Karen conceded. "For turnover and engagement, the only criterion I wrote into Laurie's plan was the word 'improvement.' I guess that's not really much of a measurement."

"Exactly," Maria said. "That's why Laurie can brag about meeting the requirements with a two-point improvement in turnover and a three-point improvement in engagement, even though her numbers are well below company averages and well below what we would like to see from her department." Maria was starting to feel bad that they were talking about Laurie as if she weren't there.

"And when I wrote, 'improvement in the area of talent acquisition,' there was really no measurement built in at all," Karen admitted.

Laurie felt compelled to rejoin the conversation. "So are you guys saying that I've been doing a bad job this year?"

Maria chuckled. "Not at all." She said. "We're saying that we have done a bad job. We wanted to hold you responsible for some pretty important aspects of your job, but we failed to say how we would measure your success. It's a direct violation of one of my Talent Management Principles. You simply cannot have accountability without clear goals and objective measurement. Performance reviews should not be based on subjective interpretations by managers."

Talent Management Principle Number 6

If you're going to hold people accountable, you must provide clearly articulated, measurable standards. There is no accountability without measurement.

"So now you're saying that I have been doing a good job?" Laurie asked. She wasn't really following.

Maria loved that Laurie lived in a black-and-white world. "Actually, Laurie, what I'm saying is that we need to figure out the best ways to measure whether you're doing a good job," she said.

Karen, who was following, said, "So measuring things like billable hours and profitability is pretty easy…"

"Yes," Maria agreed, "and those are still important parts of Laurie's job."

"But," Karen continued, "figuring out appropriate measures for retention and engagement is a bit harder. And figuring out how—and when—to measure hiring is really hard."

"Yes, I agree that it is really hard," Maria said. "But there's a difference between really hard and impossible. It's not impossible. Our challenge as managers is to figure out how to measure the things that are important for our business. Once we figure out the appropriate ways to measure things, holding people accountable becomes a lot easier."

Laurie said, "This meeting didn't really go as I had anticipated."

Karen apologized, "I'm sorry about that."

Maria agreed. "Me too. But working together, the three of us are going to figure out what's important in your job and how to measure it. Once we do that, I can assure you that your performance reviews will have no surprises. They will be based on previously agreed-upon measurements."

"Good." Then Laurie turned to Karen and said with a smile, "So then can we do my performance reviews without Maria?"

Simultaneously, Maria and Karen said, "Yes!"

Organizational Assessment

	NOT AT ALL		NEUTRAL		TO A GREAT EXTENT
1. To what extent does your organization focus on long-term goals instead of focusing on short-term (quarterly or annual) goals?	1	2	3	4	5
2. To what extent does your organization give employees measurable, quantitative targets instead of general goals such as "improve"?	1	2	3	4	5
3. To what extent does your organization measure the quality of hire based on performance on the job as opposed to time, cost, or credentials?	1	2	3	4	5
4. To what extent does your organization generally measure the right, meaningful metrics regarding business outcomes?	1	2	3	4	5
5. To what extent does your organization generally know how to measure the right, meaningful metrics regarding employee performance?	1	2	3	4	5
6. Are employees evaluated and held accountable based on objective quantitative measures as opposed to subjective perceptions from managers?	1	2	3	4	5
7. Is your organization able to evaluate functions like talent management with the same rigor that it uses to measure outcomes like sales and profits?	1	2	3	4	5

Questions for Personal Reflection

1. Was there anything described in chapter 6 that seemed descriptive of your organization?

2. Do you tend to focus on long-term organizational goals or short-term objectives?

3. When you hire people, do you evaluate the success of your hiring based on actual performance on the job? If so, what is an appropriate time interval to wait before you are able to adequately assess performance of a new hire?

4. As an employee, have you ever felt that you were being evaluated subjectively (and perhaps unfairly)?

5. When you evaluate the performance of others, do you use objective, quantifiable measures or subjective perceptions?

6. What would be some appropriate measures of success in your job? Have you discussed these with your manager?

K aren Michaels, the chief operating officer, burst into Maria's office. "What is this!?" Maria ignored her.

"Maria, I'm talking to you."

"No you're not," Maria said. "You're yelling at me. You're not my parent and you're not my boss, and I don't respond to people who talk to me in that tone of voice." Civility in the workplace had become an issue for Maria and she didn't want Capital View to be a place where people spoke to each other like that. She definitely wasn't going to let it be a place where people spoke to her like that.

"Well, there's something we need to talk about."

"Then let's talk. Please calm down and have a seat."

"I'm sorry for the tone," she said. "But I tend to get angry whenever I see this company wasting money."

"OK, I'll bite. Where do you think we're wasting money?"

"I've been looking over the proposed budget, and I saw that you want to expand our training and development budget by more than 40 percent."

"That's right," Maria said calmly. She could see Karen was getting excited again and didn't want to add fuel to the fire.

"I don't know if you've been able to keep up with our financials, but revenues are flat. We need to cut costs, not spend more."

"Karen, I am perfectly capable of keeping up with the financials." Maria said. Maria had observed that people tend to think that HR executives don't understand the financial side of the business. Maria had an MBA from Columbia Business School so she was more than capable, but she didn't want to dwell on that part of Karen's rant. "Given the current financial environment, I think the budget for learning is more than justified."

"How can you say that?" Karen started raising her voice again. "With flat revenues, spending on training is a luxury we just can't afford. I'm going to recommend to Will and Bobby that we cut the training budget, not expand it."

"Training is not a luxury. It's a necessity. And I would argue that in tough financial times, it becomes more important, not less."

"That's insane and I'm not going to let this happen."

"It's not your call."

"Maybe not, but as chief operating officer, I have a say in the budget process and I'm going to bring this issue to Will and Bobby."

"Why don't we see if they're available now and we can see where they stand on this?" This would be a good test of Will's support and she'd love to find out where the chief financial officer's thinking was.

"I can't do it right now. I have to go talk to Regina about the marketing budget. As chief marketing officer, she's trying to increase spending on advertising. Don't you people get it? Revenues are flat—we can't increase our spending."

"Why don't we do this—let's schedule a meeting with Will, Bobby, and Regina and the five of us can discuss these issues," and then she added, pointedly, "in a calm and rational manner."

"Fine," Karen said. "Why don't you connect with my assistant and try and coordinate everyone's calendar?"

"I'll be happy to," Maria said.

The meeting was set for the following Monday morning. It was one of those late fall days in New York in which the sky was completely gray and the cold wind came whipping in from the water. Maria hoped the weather wasn't foreshadowing the tone of the meeting. At least there were bagels. That was always a good sign.

Regina Clark, the chief marketing officer, looked a bit concerned as she entered. Will, Karen, and Bobby followed her in.

Will started, "Maria, why don't you tell us why you've called this meeting?"

"Actually, Will, I've scheduled it on behalf of Karen, who has some issues about next year's proposed budget."

Will was confused. "Aren't the departmental budget meetings scheduled for next week?"

The company's annual budget process was in full swing. Department heads submitted their proposed budgets, they were reviewed by senior executives, and then meetings were held, department by department. Department heads were expected to defend their budget proposals and address questions posed by the senior executives. The company's annual operating budget was then finalized by Bobby and Will.

Karen responded, "Yes, but I've seen some of the proposed budgets and I've got some concerns that I thought should be addressed prior to the departmental budget meetings."

Maria said, "I agree. If there are some philosophical differences about how this company is going to address the lack of growth, I think we should discuss them now as an executive team prior to having the line-by-line discussions with the department heads next week." At least Maria and Karen were on the same page about the process. And it couldn't hurt to start off with some agreement, rather than butting heads at the start of the meeting.

Will understood. "Fine," he said. "Karen, what are your concerns?"

To her credit, Karen responded calmly and thoughtfully. "Will, I've been concerned that our revenues have been flat. Given the current market, I don't see much growth happening next year. To maintain our profitability, I think we need to cut costs, not increase our spending."

The CEO nodded, but didn't say anything. Bobby, the CFO, was the one who responded, "Makes sense. So what's the problem?"

Maria knew that Will would keep an open mind during this discussion. She was eager to find out where Bobby would land. Was he the type of CFO who would always look to cut costs, or would he be open to ideas that might help grow the company?

Karen continued, "When I looked at some of the proposed budgets, I was shocked that some of our departments," she looked pointedly at both Maria and Regina, "were increasing spending in certain areas where I don't think we can afford to spend extra money."

Bobby took the bait, but he did so with his characteristic impish grin, "Gee, Karen, is there any way we could persuade you to share with us what those areas might be?"

Karen either ignored or didn't pick up on Bobby's playful tone and continued, "To start, I think training and advertising are luxuries that we just can't afford to spend more on when revenues aren't growing."

Regina was visibly upset. "Luxuries?" She said. "How can you call advertising a luxury?"

Karen could see that she had touched a nerve with Regina and didn't want the meeting to be personal or confrontational. "Perhaps luxury was too strong of a word," she said. "I don't want the company to have to do layoffs—and I know Maria would agree with me there." She looked over to Maria, who just smiled and nodded. "We have to spend money on payroll. If we can't cut that, then we have to cut other places. Payroll isn't optional, but advertising is. Training is the same way—we don't have to spend money on training. When we've got the money, I'm all for spending some on training. But when money is tight, we've got to cut costs, and I think our optional spending areas should be cut, not expanded."

Regina was livid. "Wait just a minute..."

Before Karen could respond, Maria intervened, "Perhaps I can help. I think I see the source of our," she paused, searching for the right words, "philosophical differences."

Maria turned away from both Karen and Regina and turned toward Will at the head of the table. "Will, as you see it, what is the purpose of advertising?"

"Well, when done properly, advertising should bring in new business."

"And Will, in your view, what is the purpose of training and development?"

"If done properly, training and development should make our people more effective, efficient, and productive."

"So why on earth, in times of flat revenue, wouldn't we want to invest in bringing in more customers and making our people more productive?" Maria asked. By now, she had turned back to Karen and was more or less addressing the question to her.

Seeking an ally, Karen turned to the CFO. "Come on, Bobby, you've been around long enough," she said. "You know that when costs need to be cut, advertising and training are two areas that we always trim."

Bobby answered cautiously, "Yes, historically that is how we've done it in the past."

Before Karen could continue, Maria chimed in again. "I think I see the problem here. Karen is viewing our budgets for advertising and training as a cost." She said.

Karen took the bait. "I'm looking right at your budget," she said. "You are looking to spend a lot of money on training and development. If that's not a cost, then what is it?"

Maria answered without hesitation, "It's an investment."

Karen looked annoyed. "That's just semantics," she said. "This is too important to play word games."

Now it was Maria's turn to be annoyed. "Yes, it's semantics," she replied. "'Semantics' refers to the meaning of words, and meaning is important and shouldn't be trivialized or dismissed. There's a difference between a cost and an investment and if we're trying to grow the company, we need to be mindful of those differences."

Karen interrupted, "Yes, but…"

Maria continued, ignoring the interruption. She picked up the bagel she had been nibbling on. "You see this bagel? We spent money on this. When I eat this bagel, it will be gone and the money has been spent. It's a cost. The hope was that we would get some satisfaction or nutrition from it, but there's no future benefit. When we invest in advertising, there is every expectation that every dollar we spend will bring back two or three more dollars."

Regina jumped in, "Ideally it would be 10 dollars!"

"Exactly," Maria kept going. "Similarly, our training and development budget is not a luxury. The idea is that every dollar we spend on training and development will return two or three or 10 dollars in increased productivity or efficiency. So while I understand the need to cut costs during slow times, I do not at all understand the desire to cut investments. So I ask again, when revenues are flat, why on earth would we cut back on investing in areas that are designed to bring in customers and increase productivity?"

Now everyone was looking at Karen. She knew she had to respond, but wasn't quite sure where to go. She started talking and hoped an argument would emerge. "First of all, I understand the difference between a cost and investment. I guess I understand the need to increase the advertising budget." She looked at Regina.

I guess I'm off the hook, Regina thought, for the moment, anyway.

"But I've still got a problem with our training and development budget." She said and turned back to Maria. "It seems like we do a lot of training for the sake of doing training. People expect it, we promise it, and we just do it because we're supposed to. I guess I'm not seeing the two or three or 10 dollars that we're supposed to be getting back from this so-called investment."

Maria was a bit relieved. "So your issue is not so much with the idea of investing in developing our people, it's with the execution and effectiveness of our training?" She said.

"I guess that's right," Karen conceded.

"Fair enough." Now it was Maria's turn to be conciliatory. "As long as we can agree philosophically that the budget we devote to training and development should be viewed as an investment, not a cost, I'm happy."

"But," Karen began, then paused for effect, "what about the problem of our not being able to see the return on that investment?"

"It's a fair question. Suppose I could guarantee you a three-to-one return-on-investment for every dollar we devote to training and development?"

Bobby jumped in, "From a CFO's perspective, I'd love to see that!"

Will followed, "Hey, if you could do that, I'd triple your training budget!"

They all laughed.

Karen was not going to let her off the hook that easily. "Can you? Can you really guarantee a three-to-one return?"

Maria answered honestly, "I don't know. I haven't been here long enough to assess the effectiveness of our training and development efforts. But since today's meeting was about our philosophies for growth and the ideas underpinning our budget, I wanted to at least get agreement that the idea behind devoting resources to training was to increase productivity and effectiveness. That idea is so important to me that it's one of my Talent Management Principles. It ties directly to the first principle about people being our most valuable asset."

Talent Management Principle Number 7
Money spent on training and development is not a cost, it's an investment—an investment designed to increase the asset value of our most valuable resource.

Karen wasn't done. "OK, suppose I buy into your premise," she said. "What happens if we invest all this money in educating our people and they leave the company?"

Maria was anticipating this question. She had heard it many times before. In fact, there was ample research that showed that organizations that provide educational benefits had lower turnover than those that do not. In addition to the increased productivity and efficiency derived from training, increased retention is usually another benefit. But Maria didn't want to cite statistics here. She had a simpler argument.

Karen grew impatient watching Maria reflect on the question, so she asked again, "Well, Maria, what if we invest in educating our people and they leave?"

Maria responded with a question, "What if we don't educate our people and they stay?"

There was a moment or two of silence as everyone reflected on that.

That should do it, Maria hoped. Maybe this meeting is finally over.

But Karen had one more arrow in her quiver. "While we've agreed in principle that training should provide productivity and efficiency gains, we still haven't addressed the question of whether the money we're spending—excuse me—*investing* in training is actually doing us any good."

Maria knew she had a point. "You're right, but that's a bigger issue than we can address in this meeting."

"That may be so," Karen agreed, "but we still need to address it."

"Absolutely," Maria wanted to end on a point of agreement. "And I promise I will be looking into this and addressing it soon."

When she said this, Maria had no idea just how soon it would be.

Organizational Assessment

	NOT AT ALL		NEUTRAL		TO A GREAT EXTENT
1. To what extent does your organization view training as a necessary and important business process as opposed to a luxury?	1	2	3	4	5
2. During downturns, does your organization avoid excessively cutting budgets for training and development?	1	2	3	4	5
3. To what extent does your organization view the training and development function as an investment instead of a cost?	1	2	3	4	5
4. When your organization conducts training, is there a genuine belief that the goal is to improve productivity and efficiency, as opposed to just being one of those things that it's supposed to do?	1	2	3	4	5
5. Does your organization realize the true benefits of internal education programs (as opposed to being fearful that people will be educated and then leave)?	1	2	3	4	5

Questions for Personal Reflection

1. Was there anything described in chapter 7 that seemed descriptive of your organization?

2. Do you believe that the training you have received in your career has improved your performance?

3. Do you believe that the training programs you have designed or delivered have had a positive effect on individual or organizational performance?

4. What can you do to ensure that future training programs that you participate in will improve your performance?

5. What can you do to ensure that future training programs that you design or deliver will definitely have a positive impact on individual or organizational performance?

6. What can you do to help your organization view expenditures on training and development as an investment instead of a cost?

8

Maria, can you settle something for us?"

Maria had barely settled into her office after the budget meeting when Ed Eddington and Tom Washington burst into her office. She wondered why the vice president of shared services needed her help with an issue relating to her new chief learning officer.

"OK, Ed, what's going on?" She said.

"Tom wants to eliminate my leadership development program," Ed replied.

"I didn't say that," Tom said.

Temperatures were getting a little hot, so Maria intervened. "What did you say, Tom?" She asked.

"I said, we need to look at the program and consider whether it should be continued."

"It sounds like he wants to cut it to me," Ed said.

"OK, Ed, calm down," Maria said. "Let's talk through this and see if we can figure it out."

Ed calmed a bit, but still seemed agitated. As head of shared services, he had a lot of employees under him. While not involved in the revenue generating aspects of the business, most of the support staff reported to Ed. He was very protective of his people and he had a reputation for investing in the development and advancement of them. His people liked it that when there was an opening, he promoted from within rather than looking outside. Ed himself had risen through the ranks from an entry-level accounts payable position to the vice president job. He had been with the company for more than 25 years and was universally liked.

Ed started, "It's pretty simple. We've been running our leadership development program for a long time and now Tom comes in and wants to look at cutting it. Maria, I know you're big on investing in people, so I know I can count on you to nip this in the bud and let me continue with my program, right?"

"Well, you're right that I believe in investing in people, but I can't give you carte blanche to run a program until I know a little something about it."

"What do you need to know?" Ed said. "The title says it all. It's a leadership development program for the people in shared services. Don't we want to develop the leadership capabilities of our people?"

"Not necessarily," she said.

Both Ed and Tom were surprised by Maria's answer.

"Why wouldn't we want to develop leadership capabilities?" Ed asked.

Maria answered the question with a question, "It depends—what do you mean by leadership?"

Ed was surprised by the question. "You know, leadership." He said.

"No, Ed, I really don't know. The term *leadership* means a lot of different things to a lot of different people."

Ed was getting confused. "I think we all have a general idea of what leadership is." He said. "And whatever words we choose to define it, can't we all agree that it's a good thing? And that more of it is better?"

Maria knew this was going to take a while, but patience was one of her virtues. "First of all, I'm not sure that a general idea is good enough," she said. "There are hundreds of books on leadership published every year and they all define it differently. If we're going to invest a lot of money and even more resources in terms of people being away from their jobs and in a classroom, I think we should at least be aware of what the course is trying to teach beyond a vague, general notion of leadership. Ed, I assume you've sat in on some of the sessions at this leadership development program?"

"Yes, I have," he said.

"So how would you define leadership?"

Ed thought for a moment. He knew he had to be careful here. "Well, at its most fundamental level, leadership means the ability to lead."

Maria smiled. He was right about that. "That's a good start," she said. "But now I have to ask, what does it mean to lead?"

Ed knew that was coming. "I guess it means getting people to accomplish goals."

Maria had more questions. "Isn't that a description of what 'management' is?" she asked.

"I'm not sure I know what you mean." Ed said.

"Ed, you have people reporting to you. Your job as a manager is to get your people to accomplish goals. For some people who might need motivation, you can motivate them with rewards or consequences. For most people, you probably just have to set the goals and objectives, make sure they have the proper resources, and then just keep an eye on things to make sure the jobs get done."

"Yes…"

Maria continued, "That's management. In your leadership development classes, I'm sure you teach more than having managers make sure their employees get the work done."

Now Ed was starting to understand. "Sure," he said. "In fact, one of the things we teach in the leadership development program is that leadership has nothing to do with where your job happens to fall on the organizational chart. Anyone can be a good leader, regardless of positional authority. As a matter of fact, that's one of the primary goals of the program. We want to have leaders at all levels. Our goal is for everyone in shared services to be a leader."

"If everyone is a leader, who's going to follow?" Maria asked.

"Huh?" Ed said, confused again.

"Ed, you said earlier that at its most fundamental level, leadership means the ability to lead. But in order to lead, someone must follow. Does this sentence make any sense: 'I'm a great leader, but no one is following me'?"

"Not really."

"We invest so much in teaching people how to lead, that we forget to teach them when to lead. There's a time to lead and a time to step back and let others lead. We really don't want everyone in the organization trying to lead all the time."

"OK, Maria, I get that. But wouldn't you at least agree that it's a good thing to make sure our people have the ability to lead, either for those times when they need to or perhaps as they advance in the organization?"

"Again, not necessarily."

"Why the hell not?"

Oops. She had been trying to calmly get Ed to understand her point, but she hadn't made it yet and Ed was more annoyed than ever.

"OK, Ed, let's back up a minute," she said. "Would you agree that we're investing a lot in this leadership development program?" She was careful to use the word invest rather than spend.

"Yes."

"How much are we investing each time we offer the program?"

"I don't have the exact figure, but I can get it for you."

"Without getting me the exact figures, can you tell me what the various expenses are?"

"Well, there's the cost of the facilitator. We also provide some books and materials. There's a continental breakfast, lunch every day, and cookies in the afternoon."

"How long does the program last?"

"It's a three-day program."

"And how many people are in it and how often do you run it?"

"We've been doing it twice a year, and we've got 20 people in each class."

"Ed, wouldn't you agree that the salaries and benefit costs for 20 people being in class instead of on the job would be part of the calculation of our overall investment?"

"Sure."

"So what has been our return on this investment?"

"I know we've gotten a lot of value from this class."

"How would you measure that value?"

"I'm not sure I could put a precise dollar value on it," Ed said. "Is that what you're asking?"

"A precise dollar figure would be nice. We can certainly put a price on our costs, so it would be great if we could also value the benefits. But failing that, let me ask it another way: What are the business outcomes you're trying to drive?"

"I'm not sure I know what you mean."

"This is a business, not a school. If we're teaching people something, there should be a good business reason behind it."

Ed had to think for a moment. "I guess we're trying to drive better leadership deeper into the organization."

Maria shook her head. "Better leadership is not a business outcome," she said. "We're not in business to have better leadership. Better leadership might be a means to an end, but it's not an end unto itself. So let me ask again, what are the business outcomes that might derive from having better leadership deeper into the organization?"

"Are you asking me to prove conclusively that our leadership development program makes the company more profitable?"

Now he's getting it. "Ed, greater profitability would be a terrific outcome for this program, but it's not the only potential business outcome. If you could demonstrate higher productivity, greater customer satisfaction, increased employee engagement, greater retention, fewer errors—any of these things might be a desirable business outcome."

"Maria, I know the program is doing us some good, but I'm not sure I can prove a direct connection to any of those outcomes."

"Ed, I think the problem here is that you can't link the program to any business outcomes because the program wasn't designed to deliver any of those outcomes. You said the program was designed to develop the leadership capabilities of our people. But that's not a business outcome."

"So you don't agree that better leadership is a good thing?"

"It's a good thing if it drives business results. If there are no measurable business outcomes that result from the program, then it's just a waste of valuable resources."

"So are you telling me I've got to get rid of the program?" Ed said. He appeared to be disappointed.

"Not necessarily. I'm saying you've got to figure what business outcomes the program is trying to drive. If you can define those outcomes—and measure them—then the program is a keeper. But if you can't define the desired business outcomes, then there's no reason to continue doing the program."

Now Ed looked more thoughtful than disappointed. "I'm going to have to think about that. I'm not sure if I can do it, but I'll give it a try."

Ed and Tom got up to leave. They thanked Maria for her time.

"Guys, thanks for coming in. I think this was an important and useful conversation." She added, "Tom, can you stick around for a minute?"

When Ed had left the office, Tom started to speak, "Thanks, Maria, for helping to clarify this for Ed. That's exactly what I meant when I told him we needed to look at the program."

"You may not be so grateful when you hear what I have to say next."

"Uh-oh." Tom realized he said that out loud.

"I'm going to need you to go through the same process for every course, program, and initiative that your department is doing or proposing."

"That's a tall order," he said.

"Yes, it is. But I promised the executive team that training and development is an investment, not a cost."

"I'm on board with that."

"So for everything we do in training and development, we need to demonstrate a return-on-investment."

"How do we do that?"

"Well, for starters, we need to define the desired business outcome for everything we do in training and development."

"I guess we can do that. What if we discover there are programs like Ed's that don't have a predetermined business outcome?"

"I think you know the answer to that question," Maria said. "We need to either see if there really is an underlying business outcome, or, if there really isn't, then we need to cut it."

"Fair enough." Tom knew that wasn't all there was to it. "But you said 'for starters'…"

"Yes. After we determine what the desired business outcome is, we need to determine how to measure whether we're achieving that outcome."

"But isn't measurement really hard?"

"Usually not," Maria said. "If you can clearly define the desired business outcome in advance, then figuring out if we've achieved the goal usually isn't difficult. And if you can't clearly define the business outcome in advance, then measurement isn't your problem."

"But what if we can't definitively prove cause and effect?"

"What do you mean?"

"What if I can't prove that my training initiative was the direct cause of the business outcome? There are a lot of variables that drive our various business outcomes."

"True. But, Tom, if you design a program to improve one of our business metrics, and you deliver the program, and then we see improvement in that area, then that's good enough for me. And it will have to be good enough for our executive team. We can demonstrate correlation. We can't always prove causation, but I don't think we have to."

"And I assume the flip side is true?"

Maria knew where he was going with this. "Yes, I would say if you design a program to improve a certain area of the business and, after delivering the program, there is no demonstrable improvement, then we would have to conclude that the program did not succeed."

"But sometimes it takes time for the learning to translate into behaviors and for those behaviors to have a measurable impact on business results."

"Absolutely. So moving forward, for every program or initiative you offer, you need to clearly state upfront what the desired business outcomes are, what the metrics will be, and what the timeframe will be for measuring and seeing results."

"For every program?"

"Absolutely and without exception. What's the point in running any program without having a desired business outcome? And if you do have a desired business outcome, we should be able to see the results."

"You know this is really going to shake up how this company does training and development, don't you?"

"Yes, but this is vitally important. I've convinced the executive team that our training and development function is an investment, not a cost. That's one of my Talent Management Principles. But it's not enough to stand on its own. That's why it leads into my next principle."

Talent Management Principle Number 8

If you're going to treat training and development as an investment, then you must be able to demonstrate a return on that investment. That means that every program should be designed to deliver a specific business result and should be held accountable for achieving that result.

"But is it really necessary for us to show a return-on-investment for everything we do?" Tom asked.

"I think it is," Maria said. "Someone like Karen is always going to ask what our return-on-investment is, especially for a department like training and development that hasn't had to justify itself in the past."

"But Karen's a pain in the neck." He said.

Maria smiled and replied. "Yes, but that doesn't make her wrong." She continued, "Think about Bobby. His job as CFO demands that he seeks a positive return for every capital investment that this company makes. We should be no less demanding about our investments in our human capital."

Tom knew she was right. "You realize you've made my job a lot harder."

"It's not just your job, Tom. It's mine as well." She then added with a smile, "I guess that's why we get paid the big bucks."

Organizational Assessment

	NOT AT ALL		NEUTRAL		TO A GREAT EXTENT
1. Do the people in your organization have a common, universally understood definition of the word "leadership" within the context of your organization?	1	2	3	4	5
2. To what extent does your organization view leadership as a means to an end as opposed to an end unto itself?	1	2	3	4	5
3. To what extent does your organization have clearly articulated business goals that are expected to be obtained from its leadership development programs?	1	2	3	4	5
4. To what extent does your organization have clearly articulated business outcomes built in upfront into the design of all of its training and development programs?	1	2	3	4	5
5. To what extent does your organization evaluate all of its training and development programs based on whether they deliver predetermined business outcomes?	1	2	3	4	5
6. To what extent does your organization hold its training and development department accountable for the delivery of business outcomes (as opposed to learning outcomes)?	1	2	3	4	5
7. To what extent does your organization know the value (either in terms of ROI dollars or business results) of its training and development programs?	1	2	3	4	5

Questions for Personal Reflection

1. Was there anything described in chapter 8 that seemed descriptive of your organization?

2. Have you ever taken part in a leadership development program? Did it make you a better leader? If yes, then how?

3. Have you been able to translate what you have learned in leadership development programs into business results? If yes, then how?

4. Have you ever taken part in a training program that had virtually no value? If so, why didn't it have value?

5. Have you ever taken part in a training program that was valuable? If so, why was it valuable?

Y ou've got to help me, Maria."

Karen Michaels was standing in the doorway to Maria's office. It was the most civil start to a conversation that Maria had seen from Karen, so she was willing to engage. Plus, in her own way, Karen was acknowledging that Maria could be helpful. It was definitely a step up from starting a conversation by accusing her of doing something wrong.

"How can I help?"

"As you know, we're in a bit of a slump," Karen said. "We just lost a major client, so I asked him why he was dropping us. He said we're just not as innovative as some of our competitors."

"That's definitely a problem," Maria replied. "But how can I help?"

"We need to hire people who are more creative. You're our people person, so I figured you would be able to help us identify and hire creativity in our applicants."

That was almost a compliment. Maria was glad Karen had sought out her help and couldn't help but be pleased that Karen saw her as someone who might have some value to add. It was too bad that Maria saw this problem a bit differently from the way that Karen perceived it.

Maria started, "Karen, let me make sure I understand. The underlying business problem is that we're starting to lose clients and perhaps we're having trouble getting new clients. The cause of this problem is that we are perceived as not being as innovative as some of our competitors. And the proposed solution to this problem is that we should hire creative people. Is that about right?"

"Yes, I think that sums it up nicely," Karen agreed.

"Well, if I accept your premise," Maria said. "I'm not sure I agree with your conclusion."

"Huh?"

"If the problem is innovation, I'm not sure the solution is to add creative people."

"Why not?"

"Because the problem seems to be innovation, not creativity."

"What's the difference? Don't they pretty much refer to the same thing?"

"Not really. There's a difference and a pretty big one."

Karen walked all the way into Maria's office and sat down. "I have a feeling this is going to become a longer conversation than I had anticipated." She added, smiling, "And at the end of it, I think I'm going to be treated to one of your Talent Management Principles."

Maria laughed. It was nice to finally have a friendly conversation with Karen. "You've got that right," she said. "Have you got a few minutes?"

"I suspect it will be more than a few minutes, but let's go. Start your lecture."

"It's not going to be a lecture. I need to ask you a few questions."

"Shoot."

"First of all, Karen, what did you mean when you said you wanted me to help you identify and hire more creative people?"

"I'm not sure I understand the question."

"Well, what do you mean when you say 'creative people'?"

"I guess I haven't really thought about it."

Maria appreciated her honesty and her willingness to talk through the problem. "What comes to mind when I use the term 'creative people'?"

"I guess at a fundamental level, the first thing that comes to mind is people who are good at stuff like art and music."

"That's what most people think of," Maria said. "But we're a financial services consulting firm. Do we really need painters and composers? Should we throw in a few poets just for fun?" They were both laughing at this. Maria continued, "So what do we really mean when we say we say we need creative people here?"

Karen chewed on this for a couple of moments. "I guess what we're really talking about is people who can think outside the box."

"What box?"

"What do you mean?"

Maria elaborated, "People are always saying they want to think outside the box, but what box are they referring to? The way I see it, the only boxes are those we put around ourselves."

Karen was thoughtful before responding. "So maybe what I mean is I want people who don't constrain themselves with boxes."

"Now you're on to something. So let's move away from the box metaphor and back into our business. What do we really mean when we say we want workers who are creative?"

Karen chewed on this for a couple of moments. "I guess what we're really talking about is hiring people who can solve problems in new ways…" she said.

"That sounds about right. So what is the underlying skill that creative people have?"

"I guess it's the ability to come up with new ideas," Karen said. "That's what creation really is. In some contexts, it can be new art or music. In our context, creativity would mean new ideas or new solutions to client problems."

"Bingo. So creativity is the ability to come up with new ideas." Maria let that sink in for a moment. Then she went on, "So the big question is, do we currently have people with this ability?"

Karen thought. As chief operating officer, the consulting divisions reported to her. She knew that the consulting teams usually did a great job. Moreover, she knew that the consultants they had were good at coming up with new ideas. "Actually, Maria, I think we've got a lot of creative people on staff."

Maria agreed, "From what I've seen, I think that's very true."

Karen seemed puzzled. "So if we've got all of these creative people, why are we getting a reputation for not being innovative?"

"Because innovation is something else."

Karen settled in. "Go on, tell me," she said.

"First let me ask you a few questions."

Of course, Karen thought.

Maria continued without waiting for a prompt. "How did you interpret it when the client said that we weren't as innovative as some of our competitors?"

"Well, I certainly didn't take it as a compliment."

"Absolutely. Clients want innovation. So what do you suppose he meant?"

"I guess that we weren't able to implement new ideas and solutions for them—at least not to the extent that they perceived our competitors would be able to."

"Aha. So what are the key words in what you just said?"

"New ideas and solutions?"

"Yes, but are you starting to see the problem here?"

"Maria, I think I know where you're going with this. I just said that we do have creative people who can come up with new ideas. But the client said we don't."

"Not exactly. According to you, the client didn't say we can't generate new ideas. He meant that we weren't able to implement new ideas."

"And you think that's the relevant distinction here?"

"Unquestionably. Like most organizations, we're full of creative people. We've got more than enough people who can come up with new ideas. That's creativity. But innovation is the ability to put new ideas to use. It sounds like our problem is that we're not as adept at implementing new ideas."

"So let me see if I get it," Karen said. "If what you're saying is true, then creativity—the ability to generate new ideas—is a term that usually applies to individuals. But innovation—the ability to implement new ideas—usually describes organizations."

"Right!"

"So is it possible that as an organization, we are full of creativity, but lacking in innovation?"

"It's not only possible, but it's likely. In fact, I think it's a common problem in organizations today. I think most organizations are full of creative people. Any organization that's good at talent acquisition has generally hired lots of people who are capable of generating new ideas, in the right circumstances. But many of these organizations lack the ability put these ideas to use. In fact, they usually think the problem is a lack of creative people, when in fact it's a systemic problem relating to the organization. "

"So what do we do?"

"What do you think we should do?"

Karen didn't even seem to mind Maria's questioning techniques. "Well, it seems like the first step would be to determine why it is that we're not innovating if we've got all of these creative people." She said.

"Exactly."

"It seems as if it's not a people problem, it's an organization problem."

"Yes," Maria cracked a big smile and said, "so can I go now?"

Karen laughed. "I wish you wouldn't."

Maria continued, "You and I need to figure out what we're doing as an organization that prevents us from implementing new ideas."

"How do we do that?"

"We talk to people."

They reconvened a week later. Maria started right in with her questioning. "So, Karen, were you able to talk to some people?"

"Yes, it was very interesting," she said. "I have some friends who I came up with in this organization, who are still working in consulting. My conversations with them were very revealing."

"What have you learned?" Maria asked.

"Three major themes emerged from my conversations. The first is that we have become an organization that is afraid to fail."

Maria smiled. "What's wrong with not wanting to fail?" she asked. "Isn't failure bad?"

"Yes, failing is bad. But being afraid to fail is even worse. If you're not willing to fail, then you're not willing to experiment or take chances. One of my friends told me about something that happened last month. Her team was working on a problem for a client. She came up with an idea that she thought would work. When she brought it to her boss, the boss agreed that it might work, but thought it was too risky. My friend was told that if the idea failed, we might lose the client. So we went with the same types of client solutions we've been implementing since I was working in consulting."

"So what's your conclusion?"

"We have become risk averse and that trait is causing us to develop a reputation for lacking innovation. It's just like we were discussing last week. My friend was creative, but when her boss shot down her idea, it was evidence that we're not innovative. We have new ideas, but we don't put them to use."

"That's too bad. What else?"

"One of my friends said she works for a boss who doesn't really welcome new ideas from her team. He said that whenever new ideas are proposed, the boss always shoots them down."

"Any idea why?"

"He's not sure. No matter what the idea is, the response is always a list of reasons why it wouldn't work. He's not sure if his boss really hates all the team's ideas or if she just wants to implement her own ideas so she can get credit for the team's successes. Either way, he said that the team has just stopped offering new ideas because they know the boss will just reject them and do things her way."

"That's too bad. It sounds like another innovation killer. So far we have risk-averse and bosses rejecting all ideas—you said there were three major themes?"

"The third one is the worst of all. It came from a friend who works for a boss who is willing to try new ideas."

"He is willing to try new ideas? So what's the problem?"

"The problem is that when a new idea fails, someone has to be blamed," Karen said. "There was a job a while back, where a brand-new client approached us for some pretty specialized investment advice. My friend said that one of her former colleagues came up with a really creative solution. Everyone, including the boss, thought it was brilliant, so they ran with it. Unfortunately, the timing of the implementation coincided with that whole mess in Europe. The client lost money and we lost the client."

"It sounds like a good idea, but a bad outcome. That happens. But I'm afraid to ask how the story ends."

"The boss wasn't going to take the heat alone for the failure, even though the failure wasn't entirely our fault. Someone had to be blamed for the loss of the client, so fingers got pointed. Remember I said my friend told me that it was a former colleague who came up with the creative idea?"

"Uh-oh."

"Uh-oh is right. In this case, the idea generator was fired."

"Let me guess—your friend said there aren't a lot of new ideas being generated from that team anymore?"

"You got it. She says that nobody ever brings new ideas to the table anymore. If people are going to be punished for new ideas that don't work out, they're just not going to open their mouths."

Maria was disappointed to hear all of this, but not surprised.

Karen continued, "Maria, as much as I hate to admit it, you were right." She was smiling when she said this. "We've got creative people here. There's no shortage of new ideas. But we've got some management practices that kill innovation. Being afraid to fail, being unwilling to implement the ideas of subordinates, and punishing failure are all ways that we discourage innovation in our company."

"It almost sounds like we have perfected some Innovation Prevention Practices. And do you think these practices are isolated to the three bosses you heard about in your conversations?"

"Sadly, no." Karen said. "I'm certain that if we talked to a lot more people, we'd see these practices throughout the organization. I think if managers are acting like this, it's because they believe that's the way the organization wants them to behave. I'm afraid the lack of innovation stems from our culture, not from a few isolated managers. Unfortunately, inadvertently, and unintentionally, we have developed a culture that stifles innovation."

"Karen, you look more sad than angry."

"I am sad, because as a senior manager in this company, I share responsibility for creating the culture of this organization."

"Don't be so hard on yourself. We are all responsible for the culture."

"Yes, but we constantly talk about how important innovation is, yet we're the ones who are killing innovation in our own organization. How could we be so stupid?"

"Karen, it's not stupidity. Inattention to culture is a common problem in organizations. Culture is a powerful and important factor, but it's invisible, so we tend to focus more on the day-to-day exigencies that are right in front of us. I believe that most organizations tend to neglect their culture. And I think one place that this inattention manifests is in the area of innovation. It's easier to assume that our people aren't creative than to see the invisible hand of our own culture stifling innovation."

"So it's not just us?"

"Hardly. This problem is so pervasive that it's one of my Talent Management Principles."

Talent Management Principle Number 9
Your organization is full of creative people who are capable of generating new ideas. As an organization, you need to find ways to implement new ideas instead of inhibiting innovation. If the organization is not innovative, it's an organizational or cultural problem, not a people problem.

"I like it," Karen said. "So what do we do about it?"

"It's simple," Maria said, grinning, "we just change the culture."

They both laughed. They finally had something they could agree on—that they had a big job ahead of them.

Organizational Assessment

	NOT AT ALL		NEUTRAL		TO A GREAT EXTENT
1. Does your organization have plenty of creative people—people who are capable of generating new ideas?	1	2	3	4	5
2. To what extent does your organization view innovation as an important initiative and a strategic priority?	1	2	3	4	5
3. How satisfied is your organization with its current level of innovation?	1	2	3	4	5
4. Does your organization avoid the common mistake of assuming that the lack of innovation is due to a lack of creative people?	1	2	3	4	5
5. Does your organization avoid the pitfall of choosing inaction out of a fear of failing?	1	2	3	4	5
6. Does your organization carefully consider new ideas from employees?	1	2	3	4	5
7. Does your organization avoid punishing failure?	1	2	3	4	5
8. Does your organization have a culture that fosters innovation?	1	2	3	4	5
9. Does your organization consciously and regularly pay attention to maintaining and growing its culture?	1	2	3	4	5

Questions for Personal Reflection

1. Was there anything described in chapter 9 that seemed descriptive of your organization?

2. Do you consider yourself to be a creative person? Why? Has your view of what it means to be creative changed after reading this chapter?

3. Do you consider your organization to be innovative? Why or why not?

4. What can you do to help your organization avoid the Innovation Prevention Practices described in this chapter?

5. What can you do to help your organization implement new ideas and be more innovative?

6. What can you do to help grow your organization's culture?

G ood cake, huh?"

Karen Michaels had come over to where Maria was standing. Now we're cake buddies? thought Maria.

"Good cake," she confirmed. "So who is it this time?"

They were at a going away party for one of Dave Marx's people. It seemed like almost every Friday they would gather in a conference room somewhere in the building to celebrate someone's retirement. Maria had begun to wonder why they never celebrated anyone's contributions to the company until their last day on the job. She typically didn't even know the person retiring, but she liked cake, so she usually showed up.

"Virgil Caine is his name."

"Did he serve on the Danville train?"

"Huh? I think he worked in tech support."

Damn, I hate working with people who are so much younger than me and don't get my musical references, thought Maria. Out loud, she said, "Never mind."

Dave Marx walked over. "How are you enjoying the cake?"

Maria thought how funny it was at these retirement parties that people talked more about the cake than the guy retiring. "Good cake. So what's Virgil's story?"

"No story, really," Dave said. "Virgil's been here forever, but he just turned 65 and decided it was time to move on to the next phase of his life."

Maria understood. "Is it just me, or have we been eating a lot of cake lately?"

Dave nodded. "You're right. We've been losing a lot of people recently. But before you can throw a Talent Management Principle at me, don't worry, it's not any kind of management issue. These are employees in their 60s who are retiring. There really isn't anything we can do to avoid this turnover."

Maria understood. She had studied the demographics of the Baby Boomers.

They were called Boomers because there was a spike in the birthrate following the return of the soldiers from World War II in 1945. From 1946 through 1964, there was a baby boom. Maria had done the math—the Baby Boomers had just started turning 65 a few years ago. While there had been an unprecedented spike in the birthrate more than 65 years ago, now they were in the midst of an unprecedented spike in the retirement rate. Maria knew that the workforce in the United States would see a wave of retirements over the next decade that had never been experienced before. She wondered how it would affect their business.

"Good cake, huh?"

Four weeks later, it was another retirement party for one of Dave's people. This time it was Bobby Rawlings who was inquiring about the cake.

"Good cake," Maria confirmed. "Who is it this time?"

"I don't know the guy. People call him Maurice."

"Because he speaks of the pompatus of love?"

"Huh?"

Maria sighed. "Never mind."

Dave Marx joined them. Before he could speak, Maria said, "Yes, Dave, it's good cake. What's Maurice's story?"

"No story," Dave said again. "He's been working his whole life and decided it's time to spend more time with his family. He's bought a place down in Florida and he's heading south."

Bobby said, "With the recent uptick in the stock market, people are suddenly noticing that they've got enough money in their 401Ks to retire. They may have been holding on for the last few years to boost that nest egg a bit, but now they feel they have enough."

Leave it to Bobby to see the financial reasons for the retirements.

"Dave, it's got to be a bit of a hardship on your department to be losing all of these people." Maria asked.

Before he could answer, Maria's sense of déjà vu was suddenly heightened when she looked up and saw Virgil Caine eating a piece of cake. "Am I crazy, or didn't we just have a retirement party for that guy a month ago?"

Dave answered, "The jury's still out on whether you're crazy, but you're right, Virgil did retire last month."

"So what's he doing here?"

"We needed some help with a project."

"Hadn't you hired a replacement for Virgil?"

"Yeah, but the kid didn't have Virgil's expertise. It was a pretty urgent client need, so we brought Virgil back on a contract basis."

Bobby jumped in, "Isn't that a bit expensive?"

"Yes, but what we could we do? We needed the guy and there was no one else who could do what we needed."

Maria thought she might need another piece of cake to get her through this conversation. As she was about to head over to the cake, she saw Elizabeth Reed getting a piece. "Wait a minute, Dave. I know that woman retired months ago. I remember her well—her retirement was my first cake party at Capital View."

"Yes, she did retire, but then we got a big project, so I brought her back for a while on a contract," Dave said.

"So let me get this straight. People retire, we go to the trouble and expense of hiring and training their replacements, and then we hire the retiree back?"

"It can't be helped. Sometimes they have some specialized expertise that our younger people lack."

"I'm not so sure that it can't be helped," Maria said, walking away.

The others recognized the look in Maria's eye and her purposeful walk. They knew they would be hearing more from Maria about this.

It was at the executive team meeting a couple of weeks later when they heard more about this. Maria had asked for 30 minutes on the agenda.

She started right in, "Will, what's the most valuable asset in our company?"

"Here we go again." Will realized that he had said that out loud. He continued, "OK, Maria, I'll play along. Our people are our most valuable asset. Did I get that one right?"

"Gold star for you, Will. When you say our people are our most valuable asset, do you mean that we've got strong people who can lift and pull a great deal of weight?"

"Of course not."

"Do you mean that they've got skilled hands and fine motor skills that can perform delicate tasks with great dexterity?"

"No."

Maria continued, "There was a time in the American economy when strong backs and skilled hands were important. But for a company like ours, at this time, what do you really mean when you say our people are our greatest asset?"

Will knew she was leading up to a point, so he wanted to answer carefully, "I guess what I'm really referring to is the knowledge that our people possess."

"Another gold star for you. What I'm getting at is the idea that, speaking very specifically, the real asset of our company is the knowledge in people's heads. Does that sound about right?"

She waited for the team to digest that. When she saw them nodding their assent, she continued. "So as managers in this company, wouldn't you agree that it's our job to manage this asset?"

Bobby answered, "Wait a minute, Maria. You're referring to knowledge as an asset and I see where you're coming from. But strictly speaking, an asset is something you own, and we don't own our workers and we don't own the knowledge in their heads."

"You're right, Bobby." Maria said. She understood his line of thinking. "Go on."

"I guess my point is that when I prepare our balance sheet, I list the assets that we own, which are money in the bank, property, plant and equipment, that sort of thing. Even though we might all believe we have the best people in the business, I can't list them as an asset because we don't own them. When I list our property, we own that and I know it's going to be there for us. But our people can leave any time."

Dave jumped in, "And frequently they do!"

Maria said, "That's my exact point and you guys are absolutely right. From an accounting standpoint, our people are not an asset that we own. But an asset is also something that has value. I think we can all agree that our people—and more specifically their knowledge—are valuable assets."

"Absolutely," Bobby agreed.

"And by virtue of the fact that we don't own our people or their knowledge, it becomes even more imperative that we do a good job of managing."

Will joined in, "Maria, I have to say that I think we do a good job of managing people. And since you've been here, you've made us even better at managing people."

"Thanks for the compliment, Will, and I would agree that this organization is pretty good at managing people. But what I'm talking about now is a little more subtle, I'm talking about managing knowledge."

Dave Marx said, "We've been through this before. We already have a knowledge management program here."

"Tell me about it." Maria knew a bit about this program, but was curious about how Dave would describe it.

"About five years ago, we came around to the notion that we had knowledge workers and that we needed to manage and capture their knowledge. Will made this a big initiative for us. He put me in charge of our knowledge management project."

"So what did you do?"

"I put my best people on it," Dave said. "I had them build a robust database that enabled anyone in the organization to input any knowledge that they had. It was designed to create a knowledge repository that anyone in the company could access. Theoretically, everyone would have access to the collected knowledge of the organization."

"Theoretically?"

It was Bobby who answered, "It didn't really work out as we had hoped. It was kind of the opposite of *Field of Dreams.* We built it, but no one came."

"What do you mean?"

It was Dave's turn. "We didn't get the level of input that we hoped for," he said. "People seemed to understand the value of sharing knowledge, but few used the system. It really bugged me because I made sure the system was as easy to use as possible. It had a simple, user-friendly interface and people needed virtually no training to begin using it—it was completely intuitive. It should have worked."

Maria responded kindly, "I don't think it was your fault, Dave."

"Then whose fault was it?"

"I think it was Will's fault."

The room fell silent. People were not accustomed to having their CEO accused of causing failures. All eyes turned to Will.

He smiled. "OK, Maria, what did I do wrong?" he asked.

"You put Dave on the job." As soon as Maria said this, Dave reddened with embarrassment.

"But you just said it wasn't Dave's fault," Will said. "Dave's great at what he does."

"I know Dave is great. It's not that he's not good at what he does. The problem is not that you picked the wrong person, it's that you picked the wrong department."

"What do you mean?"

"The problem was about managing knowledge. Dave is the chief information officer, and you asked him to build a database. There's a big difference between knowledge and data."

They were all listening intently, so Maria continued. "Computers are great at storing data. But knowledge doesn't reside in databases, it lives in the heads of our employees."

Will wasn't sure he understood. "I'm not sure I see the distinction."

"When we say our employees possess valuable knowledge, we don't just mean that they know a lot of facts. Factual knowledge is part of it, but mostly what we mean is that they know how to do something. The real value of our employees isn't just in what they know, it's what they know how to do."

"I'll agree with that," Will said.

"So while we can store facts and information in a database, capturing someone's skill set is a little trickier. The problem was never a problem of data management, that's why Dave's database never solved the problem."

"So how do we do it?" Will asked.

"I'm pretty sure everyone in this room knows how to do something. I'm fairly comfortable in assuming that we're all pretty good at doing our jobs, right?"

Bobby was always the playful one, and he went first. "I have my doubts about a few people in this room, but I'm pretty good at my job," he said.

"OK, Bobby, let's assume you are pretty good at your job. How did you get to be good at your job?"

"Well, I went to school. I majored in accounting, then I went on to get an MBA in finance."

"And did you emerge from business school capable of being the CFO of a large corporation?"

"Of course not. School taught me the fundamentals of the profession, but it took years of experience before I could become the CFO."

"So how did you really learn the job?"

"I guess it was a combination of things. I needed the schooling as a foundation, but the way I really learned the job was from years of experience working my way up and by having a couple of mentors who really showed me the ropes. My father was kind of an informal mentor who was always advising me on my career, and my predecessor as CFO really groomed me for this position."

"And how much of what you know about how to be a CFO did you learn from reading information that had been input into databases?"

Bobby chuckled. "Not much," he said.

"So as we look to capture the knowledge of our workers, we can't count on databases as the solution."

"Wait a minute." Dave was rejoining the conversation. "Bobby, aren't there some databases that you consult on a regular basis for financial information and guidelines about how to meet regulations?"

"Sure," Bobby conceded.

"I'm not saying there's no value in databases," Maria said. "In the world of knowledge management, I think databases and information technology can be a wonderful tool, but they are not the sole solution. They can be part of the solution and can be very helpful, but they can't solve all of our problems."

"But if they can be useful tools, I'm still not sure why people didn't use our database." Dave said.

"Why would they have?" asked Maria.

"Because it really would have helped out the company if they did," Dave said.

"Aha. All of us in this room spend a lot of time worrying about what's best for the company. But my guess is that most of our employees are not lying awake at night fretting about the company. We told them how the company would benefit if they shared their knowledge, but we never told them what was in it for them."

Now Karen spoke up. "I think the problem runs deeper than that," she said. "I know many of the consultants in this company feel that their knowledge base is their job security. If they know stuff that no one else does, then they feel we have to keep them around. After all, we all know that knowledge is power. When we ask them to share their knowledge, they feel like we're asking them to give up their power. If everyone else knows what they know, then they become expendable. But as long as they are the sole source of some expertise, they've got security and we continue to reward them for their expertise."

"That's great, until they leave the company and take that knowledge with them," Dave said, thinking of his recent retirees. "I have to end up hiring them back—sometimes paying them more than I did when they were here—just because they are the only ones who have the knowledge or expertise that we need."

"Let me see if I understand this," Will was trying to process the conversation. "We really want people to share their knowledge. But as an organization, we end up rewarding people for hoarding knowledge?"

"That's exactly right," Maria agreed.

"So how did we manage to get into this bind?" Will said. He really wanted to understand the nature of the problem.

Maria had an answer. "Because we really haven't been consciously recognizing that our employees' knowledge is the true value in this company. And that lack of recognition has meant that we haven't been focusing on managing knowledge."

"I just realized something," Karen said, "and it's kind of embarrassing."

Will encouraged her to continue. "Don't worry, Karen, I think we're all a bit embarrassed by this."

Karen went on, "Last year, we had a client come to us with a problem. He had a need for some pretty technical advice, and we assured him we could help. When we looked at the problem, we realized that we didn't have the expertise on staff to help him. The problem required some pretty specialized technical expertise in a very arcane area of finance. We realized that there were probably only a handful of people in the world who might possess this expertise. So I hired an outside consultant who specializes in finding experts to locate someone who could help us out."

"So, did she find the expert?" Will asked.

"The good news was that after searching through the whole world, she located someone who had genuine expertise in this area. The embarrassing news was that it was someone who already worked here. The expert was someone who happened to work in Bobby's finance department, so our consulting division didn't know he existed."

"Wait a minute," Will was dumbfounded. "We hired a consultant to look all over the world to find someone who was in our own building?"

"I told you it was embarrassing," Karen said.

"How could this happen?"

They all looked at Maria for the answer.

"I don't think this problem is all that uncommon or isolated to our organization," she began. "When organizations become as large and complex as ours, it's hard to keep track of who knows what."

"Yes, but size shouldn't be an excuse," added Will.

"It's not an excuse," was Maria's response, "but it does help to explain the nature of the problem."

Naturally, the CEO asked, "So what's the solution?"

"The first part is that we need to recognize the value of our workers' knowledge. Then we need to communicate to our managers that this is the wealth of our organization and they are the stewards of this asset."

Will nodded. "We can certainly get started on that."

Maria continued, "The next part is a little harder. We need to stop inadvertently rewarding people for hoarding knowledge. We need to start rewarding people for sharing knowledge."

"How do we do that?"

"I think it might start with monetary rewards," she said. "Maybe we pay people for entering some knowledge or expertise into Dave's database. But there are other ways. If we pay to send people to conferences, we need to make sure that they understand they have an obligation to share what they've learned with their colleagues. We can set up lunch-and-learn sessions where we buy pizza and make sure that someone gets up and shares some expertise. And when we have workers who are getting close to retirement, we need to make sure that their final months with us are spent mentoring younger workers, sharing what they know, and ideally training their replacements. And finally, we need to abolish the practice of hiring back our retirees. If our managers know that they absolutely, positively cannot hire these people back, they might be a little more careful about ensuring that these workers share their expertise before they leave the company."

Will nodded. "I agree with these practices, but it sounds like a big job."

"It is. It really involves changing the mindset of our company and our managers. That's why we might need financial rewards upfront. Once people see the value in knowledge sharing, we might be able to do away with financial inducements, but for now, what I'm really talking about is a culture change. We've got to change from a culture that rewards knowledge hoarding to one in which knowledge sharing becomes part of our day-to-day lives and is a vital part of our culture. I would agree that we have a long way to go to get there."

Will said, "We have to make this a priority. I think we're losing too much value when knowledge leaves this company."

Bobby added, "And we're spending too much money when we need to bring it back."

Karen said, "I think it can be even bigger than that. I know that most of our competitors are facing the same issues. If we can actually get on top of managing, collecting, and sharing our knowledge, that can be a competitive advantage for us."

Maria agreed. "You're absolutely right. The ability to manage knowledge and do it well is pretty rare and it's a great opportunity for organizations to leverage their talent and expand their capabilities. Even more importantly, organizations can become more effective and efficient, merely by doing a better job of leveraging resources that currently reside in the organization."

"Maria, I'm glad you phrased it that way," Will told her. "It's not just a problem to be solved, it sounds like a great opportunity for us, especially since as a consulting firm, we are essentially in the knowledge business."

Maria agreed. "It can be a great opportunity for any organization willing to focus on managing knowledge. And it's such a powerful concept, it's one of my Talent Management Principles."

> ## Talent Management Principle Number 10
> The wealth of an organization lies in the knowledge and skills residing in its people. The ability to manage, collect, and share that knowledge can be a competitive advantage and an opportunity to leverage value without bringing additional resources into the organization.

Three months later, Maria was eating cake again. The company had finalized its policy of no longer bringing back retired workers. Dave Marx had decided to throw a re-retirement party for the retired employees who had been working as consultants.

Maria saw Virgil Caine, Elizabeth Reed, and Maurice. As she was reflected on Dave's penchant for hiring employees with names from rock songs, she saw Dave heading toward her with another retiree. She wondered what this one's name was. Peggy Sue? Billie Jean?

Dave arrived. "Maria, I'd like you to meet our newest retiree. Her name is Eleanor Rigby."

Of course it is, thought Maria.

Organizational Assessment

	NOT AT ALL		NEUTRAL		TO A GREAT EXTENT
1. Is your organization aware of the number of retirements that it is likely to face over the next several years?	1	2	3	4	5
2. To what extent does your organization have a plan to minimize the impact of the upcoming retirements?	1	2	3	4	5
3. Does your organization avoid the practice of bringing back retired employees on contract assignments?	1	2	3	4	5
4. To what extent does your organization acknowledge that the wealth of the organization derives from the knowledge in the heads of its workers?	1	2	3	4	5
5. Does your organization behave on a regular basis as if it recognizes the value of the knowledge in the heads of its workers?	1	2	3	4	5
6. Does your organization do a good job of managing knowledge?	1	2	3	4	5
7. Does your organization do a good job of encouraging people to share knowledge?	1	2	3	4	5
8. Does your organization do a good job of capturing and storing knowledge?	1	2	3	4	5
9. Does your organization have a knowledge management program that uses methods for storing and sharing knowledge besides a database?	1	2	3	4	5
10. Do people in your organization tend to share knowledge as opposed to hoarding it?	1	2	3	4	5
11. Do the managers and executives have a good grasp of the knowledge and expertise possessed by the people in the organization?	1	2	3	4	5

Questions for Personal Reflection

1. Was there anything described in chapter 10 that seemed descriptive of your organization?

2. Do you tend to share your knowledge freely or hoard it? Why?

3. What can you do to encourage more people in your organization to share knowledge?

4. What can you do to be a better manager of knowledge?

5. What knowledge do you possess that can potentially be of value to your organization?

6. Are your organization and your manager aware that you possess this knowledge and do they leverage its value?

11

The weekly executive team meeting was winding down. Everyone was hoping to get out a bit early when Will asked, "Any new business?"

Maria started packing up her things when Dave Marx said, "Actually, I've got an issue I was hoping you guys could help with."

Maria settled back into her seat, hoping it wouldn't be a long conversation, but fearing that it probably would be.

Dave continued, "I was hoping you guys could offer some advice on how to manage workers from different generations."

Maria poured herself a big cup of coffee. She now knew this was going to be a very long discussion.

Will asked, "What exactly do you mean, Dave?"

"I've been reading a lot about the generational differences in the workplace," he said. "I've got workers from across a broad spectrum of ages in my department and I was wondering if anyone could offer any advice on this new problem of how to manage people from the various generations."

Everyone turned to look at Maria. She was glad that the executive team had started to view her as a good resource, but she really didn't want to get involved in this particular minefield. But they were all looking at her, and she knew she would have to.

She thought a good place to start would be by asking a few questions.

"Dave, before we begin, can you tell me exactly what the problem is that we're trying to solve here?"

Dave began, "I read somewhere…"

Uh-oh, Maria thought to herself. In her experience, very little good came from discussions that started with "I read somewhere." She continued listening.

"I read somewhere that for the first time in history we have four different generations all working together in the workplace," Dave said.

Maria nodded. "I'm aware of the problem," she said. "First we've got the Silent Generation—people born between 1928 and 1945. Then there are the Baby Boomers who were born between 1946 and 1964. Next comes Gen X, people from 1965 to roughly the early 1980s. Now we've got Gen Y or Millennials entering the workforce, people born after the Gen X group."

Karen looked puzzled. "So what exactly is the problem here?" she said.

Maria explained, "People in each of these groups tend to have different characteristics. For example, Baby Boomers tend to be reluctant to adopt new technologies, and Millennials tend to be less loyal to their employers. Also, there is the problem of communication styles and the ability for all of these generations to get along. I've read that this is becoming an increasingly larger problem in the workplace."

Karen seemed agitated. "Maria, I would have thought you of all people would be immune to jumping on the bandwagon of the so-called generational problem."

"You don't think this is a real problem?" Maria asked.

"I think we're creating problems where they don't exist."

Maria was interested in where Karen might be going with this. "Can you walk us through your reasoning?" she asked.

"Gladly." Karen began, "First of all, I keep hearing that we have four generations side-by-side in the workplace for the first time in history. This is nonsense. Yes, the Silent Generation workers are about 65 or older and still in the workplace. The Boomers are roughly in their 50s and 60s. The Gen X people are in their 30s and 40s and the Millennials are under 30. But how is this new? It's not like a generation ago when I joined the workforce everyone was 42 years old. We've always had people in their 20s, 30s, 40s, 50s, and 60s working side by side. The only thing new is that now, for the first time, we have attached labels to the various generations."

Maria contemplated this. "I never thought of it that way."

"Look at it this way," Karen said. "The reason we created the category of Baby Boomers is because of the spike in the birth rate that began in 1946 and ended in 1964. Because we had suddenly attached a label to this group, we felt a need to name the next group. So we came up with the not-so-creative name of Generation X. We were even less creative in calling the one that came after that Generation Y. And we retroactively labeled the pre–Baby Boom generation the Silent Generation."

"Anyone who had ever met my father certainly wouldn't have affixed that label to him," Bobby added with a chuckle.

"And that brings me to my next point." Karen said, she was picking up steam now. "We have been guilty of stereotyping people based on what generation they fall into. Stereotyping in general is a dangerous practice, but in this case I think it leads down some very bad roads."

"I really hadn't realized we were doing that," Maria confessed.

"You yourself just said that older workers tend to not embrace technology and that younger workers tend to not be loyal." Karen said. "That's some pretty broad stereotyping. As the chief people officer, would you ever allow anyone in this company to stereotype based on other demographic characteristics? What if someone started to say, 'Compared to white people, people of color tend to be...'"

"I would shut them down before they could complete the sentence," Maria said quickly.

"Of course you would, and rightly so. And what if someone said, 'Compared to men, women tend to be...'"

"I've got this," Bobby jumped in. "Smarter, right?"

Everyone laughed, but Maria said, "Karen, you're right. We don't allow stereotyping based on all kinds of demographic characteristics. But apparently it's become commonplace for everyone—including me—to stereotype based on age."

Dave rejoined the conversation. "But aren't some stereotypes based on truth?"

"Perhaps," Karen responded, "but by lumping people in groups, we tend to lose focus on individual differences. There are two problems here. First, by drawing lines between the groups, we place people in categories that don't always make sense. I was born in 1963, so that makes me a Baby Boomer. My sister was born in 1965, so she's Generation X. This type of categorization would imply that I might share more characteristics with a fellow Baby Boomer who was born in 1946 than with my own sister who is only two years younger."

Dave responded, "I can see that, but you said there are two problems."

"Yes," she said. "The other is that by assuming people possess certain traits and characteristics based on their group, we make assumptions about individuals that may be far from the truth. One of the most common of these so-called generational differences is that older workers tend to not embrace new technologies the way younger workers do. While there may be some truth to this if we look at the issue very broadly, when we as managers of individuals focus on the stereotype, we may draw some very wrong conclusions, right Dave?"

She had singled out Dave for this example because he was the oldest person in the room at 64 years old. Yet Dave had the reputation of being not only the most tech-savvy person at Capital View, but one of the technology leaders on Wall Street.

"Sorry, I didn't hear you, Karen," Dave quipped. "I was busy writing an app for my new tablet."

"The other stereotype I keep hearing is that Millennials are less loyal to their companies than workers from other generations."

"Wait a minute, Karen." Dave said. "I think there's some truth to this one. When I look at the turnover statistics from my department, I definitely see more turnover from the younger workers than the older ones."

"That might be true, but it's not necessarily a defining trait of the generation. Workers of all generations tend to show their employers about the same amount of loyalty that the employer shows them. Our parents and grandparents had employers who told them to show up and work hard, and if they did that, they would have a job for life. Are we offering that deal to our younger workers?"

"Hardly," Will answered. "We've become pretty cavalier about bringing people on and then letting them go." He was becoming increasingly concerned that Capital View had started going on hiring binges when client work was plentiful, and then downsizing when things changed. After a few cycles of this, he was worried about how morale might be affected.

"Exactly. It wouldn't be reasonable for us to expect our younger workers to be more loyal to us than we have been to them. We have been loyal to our older workers, but the Millennials see us hiring a lot of people and then letting them go, so why should they be loyal to us? But instead of looking at the underlying reason for their lack of loyalty, we tend to attribute it to a generational trait. In short, people tend to leave companies if their desires or needs are not being met."

Bobby chimed in. "Hold on. What do you mean when you say, 'Their desires or needs are not being met?' We compensate them for their work and in some cases we pay them quite well."

Karen answered, "People come to work for reasons in addition to the paycheck. Our parents and grandparents wanted stability, security, and possibly a chance to move up the corporate ladder. I've come to learn that modern workers sometimes value flexibility more than money, and they increasingly desire work that is meaningful or challenging. That's why I think we need to look at our relationship with our younger workers and figure out what we can do to earn their loyalty instead of blindly expecting it or dismissing the lack of it as a generational characteristic."

Will responded, "Karen, this has been very helpful, but can you help us address the problem of how to manage workers from different generations?"

"Yes—by not viewing it as a problem."

"What do you mean?"

"When women started joining the workforce in numbers nearly equal to men, we viewed this as a positive development," she said. "We actively recruit people of color because we feel that having a more diverse workforce will benefit us as a company as well as our clients. In every demographic category that I can think of, we view diversity as a benefit. But every time I hear someone discuss the generational diversity in our workforce, I hear it presented as a problem!"

"Wow," Will said. "I never thought of it like that, but now that you've mentioned it, Karen, I think we've all been guilty of this, myself included."

Karen continued, "I think we need to reframe the problem. The problem is not that we have workers from different generations; the problem is determining how we can best leverage this diversity in our workforce. In other words, how can we benefit from having workers from different age groups?"

Will was thoughtful. "I can see where you're going with this," he said. "There are certainly things our older workers can teach our younger workers and vice versa. I have just one concern about this conversation. Maria has been uncharacteristically quiet."

Will was right. Maria had been silent for much of the dialogue. She was scribbling in her notebook when Will's mention of her name got her attention.

"Sorry, everyone," Maria said quietly. "I have been genuinely humbled by this conversation. This is a major people issue, and I really hadn't thought it through very thoroughly. I really want to thank Karen for her insights and for bringing all of us—including me—up to speed on this issue."

"Thanks, Maria." Karen said, she really appreciated the compliment. "I'm surprised you didn't have a Talent Management Principle about this issue."

"I didn't," Maria confessed, "but I do now." Maria revealed what she had been writing during the meeting. "Thanks to Karen, I am happy to present a new principle!"

Talent Management Principle Number 11

Having four different generations in the workforce is not a new problem. It's not new—there have always been workers in a wide range of ages working together. And it's not a problem—it's another form of diversity that can be a valuable asset if managed properly.

Dave added, "Thanks for clarifying this issue for me. Would I be succumbing to an age stereotype if I said I'm tired of sitting here and would love for this meeting to be over?"

Bobby answered, "I think a desire to end meetings is something people of all age groups can agree on."

Organizational Assessment

	NOT AT ALL		NEUTRAL		TO A GREAT EXTENT
1. Do the executives in your organization view having workers from different generations as a diversity opportunity as opposed to a management problem?	1	2	3	4	5
2. Do people in your organization avoid stereotyping based on age or generational group?	1	2	3	4	5
3. Has your organization become aware of higher turnover from younger workers than those in other age groups?	1	2	3	4	5
4. Has your organization investigated the root causes of younger worker turnover as opposed to attributing it to a lack of loyalty or some other generational characteristic?	1	2	3	4	5
5. Does your organization acknowledge that workers from different generations have different needs and desires in the workplace?	1	2	3	4	5
6. Has your organization structured its total rewards (compensation, benefits) and employee policies and procedures to reflect the different needs and desires of its workforce?	1	2	3	4	5

Questions for Personal Reflection

1. Was there anything described in chapter 11 that seemed descriptive of your organization?

2. Have you ever stereotyped or made a generalized conclusion about someone based on their age?

3. Have you ever viewed the different generations of your organization's workforce as a problem?

4. What can you do to leverage the value from having a workforce that is diverse in age?

5. As an employee, what (other than money) do you value and hope for from your employer?

6. What do your colleagues and direct reports value and hope for from their employer?

H ow's it going so far?" Will inquired of his executive team at the weekly meeting.

"Not well."

"A little slow."

"Not as well as we had hoped."

"It sucks."

The company had restructured several weeks ago. The executive team had been enthusiastic that the restructuring would streamline operations and make everything work more smoothly, and, for once, they were united behind an initiative. The division heads who were consulted were unanimous in their agreement with the plan. It seemed like a perfect plan, but now Will was hearing that it wasn't going well.

"I'm surprised to hear this," he said. "I thought we had a pretty good plan in place, and now you're all telling me it's not working. Let's start with Bobby. Your response seemed to, um, express the most concern." (The "It sucks" belonged to Bobby.)

"Well," Bobby said. "I explained the change to everyone in my division. I explained the rationale behind the change. I explained the implementation plan and timetable. Finally, I ascertained their understanding."

"This all sounds good," said Will.

"I thought so too."

"So what's the problem?"

"The problem is, it sucks."

"Can you be a little more specific?"

"OK," Bobby grinned, "it really sucks."

"Come on, Bobby." Will always appreciated his CFO's sense of humor, but he was getting a bit impatient. "What's really going on?"

"What's really going on," Bobby said, back in his serious mode, "is that people are just ignoring the change. Despite my best efforts to inform, cajole, and induce them, everyone is still pretty much doing things the old way."

"That's exactly what's happening in my shop," said Dave.

"Same here," said Regina.

"I'm afraid to say I've got the same problem," said Karen.

Will turned to his chief people officer, "Maria?"

"I have to concur," she said. "It's happening in my department and I'm seeing it all over the company. I hate to say it, but our big initiative just didn't take."

Will was stunned. "This sucks," he said.

"Told 'ya," Bobby said, he wasn't happy to be right in this case.

"So what do we do?" asked Will.

"I say we make it clear to everyone that this restructuring is going to happen," Karen said. "We tell them again, but this time we make the consequences for noncompliance very clear." She was getting a bit worked up. "We make sure that everyone knows that if they continue to do things the old way, they will get written up. If people still aren't complying after a couple of warnings, maybe we need to terminate someone to send the message. We can't just have people ignoring initiatives that come from the top. It's disrespectful, it destroys our chain of command, and we just can't allow it."

The conference room fell silent, but Maria was shaking her head. Will turned to her. "Maria, do you have an alternative plan?"

Everyone turned to Maria hopefully. She thought for a moment before answering. "I'm not sure I have a fully formulated plan, but I do have an approach." She didn't wait for any inquiries before continuing. "I think before we do anything, we need to figure out why our plan isn't being implemented."

Karen jumped in. "I think the only plausible conclusion as to why our staff would ignore us is that they don't respect us."

"I disagree," said Maria. "I think the reasons are a bit more subtle. I don't think they disrespect us at all. As a matter of fact, I don't think the poor implementation has anything to do with how they feel about us."

Before Karen could respond, Bobby intervened. "Well, I'm glad to hear that they might not hate us as much as we think. But if it's not about us, then the only remaining conclusion is that they didn't believe in our plan."

"That's possible," Maria answered, "but that may not be it either."

"I don't get it." Will was clearly frustrated. "If it's not us and it's not our plan, then what could it be?"

"It might just be a reluctance to change," answered Maria.

"I get that sometimes people are resistant to change," Will responded, "but this is a good idea and pretty much everyone agreed that it's a good idea. Why would people resist a good idea?"

"It's not about the idea at all, it's about change."

"So you're saying that people aren't good at change?" Will asked. "Isn't that a pretty negative view of people?"

"Actually," Maria answered, "I think people are good at change. People change when they have a reason to change. They're good at change if they want to change or if they need to change."

Karen interrupted, "But didn't we just give them a bunch of good reasons to change?"

"No," Maria responded. "We gave them a bunch of good reasons why the organization would be better off if they changed. We didn't tell them how they would be better off. So I guess what I'm saying is that people are good at change, but they don't always like it. People change when they have a good reason to, but otherwise they tend to resist change."

"Wait a minute, Maria," Dave said, he was getting interested, "I'm just a tech guy, but you're the people person. Are you saying that all people resist all change, no matter how positive the change is?"

"Not exactly."

"Then what are you saying?"

"I'm saying many people tend to resist change, at least at first."

"But why?" Dave and Will both asked simultaneously.

"There are a lot of complex reasons," was the best Maria could come up with.

"Come on, Maria," Will said, "you'll have to do better than that. You said the best approach would be to figure out why our plan isn't being implemented. I'm sure you have some ideas as to why people resist change. Walk us through your thinking on this."

"OK. Let's see if we can work through this together." Maria said thoughtfully, "I think deep down, what causes our resistance to change is fear."

"Why would people be afraid of a good idea?" Will asked, he couldn't let go of the notion that the restructuring was a good idea.

Maria answered, "It's not about the merits of the idea. What is it that you think people are most afraid of?"

Everyone had some thoughts about this.

"Snakes."

"Death."

"Public speaking."

"Clowns." Of course this one came from Bobby.

Maria slowed them down. "Yes, these are all things that people are afraid of—and we should be afraid of all of these things," she gave Bobby a smile. "But there is one almost universal fear that people share that hasn't come up yet, and it's highly relevant to this conversation."

The room fell silent as everyone thought for a moment.

It was Karen who practically jumped out of her seat. "Fear of the unknown!" she shouted.

"That's exactly what I was thinking," said Maria. "People tend to fear the unknown. Even though we might think the idea is a good one, if it represents a change, which to many people represents the unknown, and that can be a little frightening. Even the people who are always grousing that everything around here is wrong have figured out how to get through the day. When we change something, it might get people out of their comfort zone and trigger their fear of the unknown. So even an idea that might seem like an improvement is perceived as being different, and people might, either consciously or unconsciously, resist it."

"But isn't it a good idea to get people out of their comfort zones?" Karen asked.

"Yes," Maria agreed, "but it can take time."

They all thought about this for a moment. It was Will who spoke first. "OK, that makes sense. So what do we do?"

Karen answered first. "I think we need to give them more information. If we can convince them that the change is for the better, I think they will be less likely to fear and resist it."

Everyone looked at Maria, assuming she would have an opinion on this. As usual, she did not disappoint. "I think the last thing we need to give them is more information," she said. "The resistance is usually not about a lack of understanding."

"But if we can convince them…"

Maria cut Karen off. "And it's not about making a compelling business case."

"I disagree." Karen continued. "I believe our people are quite rational, and if we make a good business case, they will come around. I think it's imperative for any type of change that we make a good business case. Are you saying that our people are not rational and that we don't need to make a good business case?"

"Not at all. I think the business case is necessary, but it's not sufficient."

"I'm not sure I understand what you mean." Karen wasn't being argumentative; she was genuinely curious.

"Let me see if I can explain. True or false, people have a logical, rational side?"

"True."

"True or false, people have an emotional side?"

"True," Karen conceded.

"True or false, people have a spiritual side?"

"True."

"And true or false, here at work, we pretend that people are strictly logical and rational beings?"

"I guess that's true." Karen answered, and everyone else was nodding.

Maria let it sink in for a moment. Before she could continue, Will spoke, "I guess you're right. We do tend to act as if people leave the emotional and spiritual sides of their personalities at home when they come to work. I guess we're all more comfortable thinking that there's no place for emotion in the workplace."

Maria nodded. "I think you're right. And things would be smoother if we were all logical and rational all day long at work. But it's just not how human beings are wired. The possibility of change can trigger our fear of the unknown, and fear is an emotion."

Ever the pragmatist, Will once again asked, "So what do we do?"

This time Karen said, "I guess more information isn't the answer."

"No," said Maria. "Since the resistance is based on fear and fear is an emotion, spreadsheets, bar graphs, and pie charts aren't going to work. You can't address an emotional reaction with a logical response."

Bobby started laughing. "Just this morning, my two-year-old daughter spilled her juice and started throwing a huge temper tantrum," he said. "I tried explaining to her that her response was a disproportionate over-reaction to the minor trauma she had just endured."

Maria smiled. "And was that the exact language you used?"

"Pretty much," Bobby admitted.

"And how'd that work out?"

"About how you'd expect. My daughter continued her tantrum and my wife looked at me like I was nuts. She patiently explained to me that I can't talk a two-year-old out of a temper tantrum with CFO speak."

Karen turned to them. "So are you suggesting that our employees act like two-year-olds who are having a tantrum?"

"Not exactly," Maria chuckled a bit at the thought. "But they might be acting a bit emotional, so our best logical arguments might not carry the day."

"I hate to sound like a broken record," Will said with a bit of exasperation, "but what do we do?"

"The first step," answered Maria, "is to acknowledge the emotion."

"How do we do that? Do we come right out and ask them what they're afraid of?" Will asked.

"Not exactly. Many people aren't even aware that it might be fear that's driving their resistance. And most people don't like to admit to us or to themselves that they're afraid."

Bobby suddenly stood up. He put his hands on his hips and said in the most macho voice he could muster, "I'm not afraid of anything!"

Everyone laughed, including Maria. "Exactly! Bobby's right. Most of us won't admit to being afraid. Especially macho dudes like Bobby." He sat down as Maria continued. "So we have to be a bit more subtle. We need to discuss our new initiatives with people, not push our ideas down their throats. And when we present a new idea, we need to ask people if they can tell us what their concerns are."

"Hold on," said Karen. "Are you suggesting that when this executive team makes a decision that's best for the company, we need ask for input from our subordinates?"

"That's exactly what I'm suggesting."

"But it's our job to make these kinds of decisions."

"Yes, but it's their job to implement the policies. If they don't buy in to our initiatives, the implementation is not going to go so well."

"So we've got to ask permission from all of our employees to implement any new policies around here?" Karen did not like where this discussion was going and she was becoming a bit agitated.

"Calm down, Karen," Maria said. "I'm not saying we need to ask permission of every employee for every new initiative."

"Then what are you saying?"

"I'm saying that we should discuss each new initiative with those employees who will have to implement the initiative or who will be affected by the initiative. First of all, they might have some legitimate concerns that we hadn't thought of. More importantly, they're much more likely to successfully implement our initiatives if we have these individual conversations."

"But won't that take a long time?"

"Absolutely."

"So won't that drastically slow down the implementation of all of our change initiatives?"

"Not really. Our employees' resistance is what drastically slows down our change initiatives. As a matter of fact, the resistance can completely stall our implementation. Look at the restructuring." Maria thought it was time to bring them back to the issue at hand. "We announced it weeks ago, and we really haven't made any progress in implementing it. Yes, it takes more time to have these conversations, but by acknowledging that people have fears and concerns and helping them talk through the issues, we might be a lot more likely to successfully implement our change initiatives."

"So let me see if I understand what you're saying," Karen said. "Because people are going to resist change, we've got to build more time into the implementation plans for all of our change initiatives?"

Maria was gratified that Karen was genuinely trying to understand her rather than argue with her. "Absolutely. I think you've summed it up nicely."

"OK, Maria, bottom-line it for me," Bobby said, back in his CFO mode.

"Sure. It's one of my Talent Management Principles." Maria said.

> **Talent Management Principle Number 12**
> People tend to resist change, and this resistance is often based more on emotion than reason.
> Individual conversations can speed the change process more than making a business case.
> The successful implementation of change initiatives usually takes more time than you originally anticipate.

"Thanks, Maria," Will said. "I still think our restructuring was a good idea, but it sounds like we really dropped the ball on implementation. We've still got our work cut out for us. I suggest that we begin looking at who will be involved in implementation and who will be most affected by the restructuring and start formulating a plan to get everyone on board. Let's reconvene tomorrow and begin working on this."

They all looked tired and it seemed like a good time to wrap up the meeting.

Bobby looked at his watch and turned to Maria. "Maria, do you have any suggestions on how we can all change from being in this meeting to not being in this meeting?"

Organizational Assessment

	NOT AT ALL		NEUTRAL		TO A GREAT EXTENT
1. Do the people in your organization tend to readily accept change?	1	2	3	4	5
2. Do change initiatives in your organization tend to go smoothly?	1	2	3	4	5
3. Do change initiatives in your organization tend to get implemented in a timely fashion?	1	2	3	4	5
4. When change initiatives are announced, does your organization go beyond making the business case and also make an affective case?	1	2	3	4	5
5. Does your organization acknowledge that sometimes emotions exist in the workplace instead of pretending that people are logical and rational all the time?	1	2	3	4	5
6. Does your organization take the time to discuss change initiatives with those who will be involved in implementation and those who will be affected by the change?	1	2	3	4	5

Questions for Personal Reflection

1. Was there anything described in chapter 12 that seemed descriptive of your organization?

2. Do you tend to embrace change or resist it? Why?

3. What can you do to be more accepting of change?

4. What can you do help others be more accepting of change?

5. Looking back, can you think of a time when your fear of the unknown was triggered by the prospect of some sort of a change at work?

6. What can you do in the future to avoid your fear of the unknown from becoming a barrier to accepting or implementing change?

7. When you announce a change, do you take the time to discuss it and address concerns with all affected stakeholders?

13

Four o'clock on Friday afternoon. A time when all thoughts turn to the weekend. Bodies are still at work, but minds have long since left the building. As devoted as Maria Green was to her work, she too was not immune to weekenditis. Her last meeting of the day had long since concluded, and Maria was relaxing at her desk, contemplating a weekend full of quality time with her dogs. As much as she devoted her career to people, at the end of a long week, some time spent away from humans and with Luna, Harvey, and Hannah seemed pretty appealing. She was wondering if she should start coming up with a list of Dog Principles. That would be a much shorter list, she thought with a chuckle. Eating, running, getting affection, and sleeping are the only things that matter to dogs. If this was all she could think about late on a Friday afternoon, she should probably head home. She wasn't going to be productive in the remaining minutes of the week. As she got up to leave, her phone rang.

Damn. I was almost out of here, Maria thought.

She debated making a run for it and ignoring the phone, but her work ethic got the better of her. She had given her assistant the afternoon off to begin his weekend early, so she had to answer her own phone.

"Maria Green," she said with no enthusiasm.

"Maria, it's Sandra." Sandra was the no-nonsense assistant to the CEO. "Will has called an emergency meeting of the executive team."

"When?"

"Right now," she said. "He needs you in the conference room right away."

"I'm on my way."

Maria wondered what it could be. She couldn't come up with any ideas, but she figured an emergency meeting called at four o'clock on a Friday couldn't possibly be a good thing. She feared her weekend might end up being spent dealing with people problems instead of dog fun after all.

She entered the conference room with some trepidation. As soon as she opened the door, she was greeted with a loud shout of "Surprise!"

It worked. Maria was genuinely surprised, and more than a little confused. She saw the cake and wondered if perhaps someone had decided to throw her a going-away party. "What's going on?" she said. "Today's not my birthday."

"No," Will said, "but it is a special day, isn't it Maria?"

I'm sure it is, Maria thought to herself, but I have no idea what it is.

Out loud, she said, "OK Will, I'll play along. What is today?"

Will laughed. "Maria, how could you not realize that today marks your one-year anniversary with Capital View?"

Wow. Had it really been a year already? Maria tended to ignore milestones like anniversaries, a character flaw that her husband found to be equal parts frustrating and endearing. She also really didn't like it when a fuss was being made about her. On the other hand, there was cake.

"Thanks, everybody," she said. "I guess I've been too busy shaking up the company to realize that a year had passed."

Will laughed the hardest. "I guess that's my fault," he said. "I challenged you to shake up the company when I hired you. I had no idea what I was getting myself into. If I had only known…"

"You would have done things exactly the same way," Bobby finished Will's thought for him.

"Yes," Will conceded, "I would have. You've done a lot of good for this company, Maria, and I want to thank you."

"I second that." Maria was shocked to hear Karen Michaels offer her a bit of praise. "I know I may have been a little resistant to some of your ideas at first."

"I've never known you to resort to understatement," Maria said, laughing.

"Fair enough," Karen said, she was laughing too. "I really didn't like the new ideas you brought to the company—at first. But I can't argue with results. I just wanted to publicly thank you for all you've done for the company."

Maria was very gratified. Not just that Will and the company had embraced her, but also that Karen, who had been her chief rival and the biggest obstacle to implementing the Talent Management Principles, had finally come around.

"Thanks, Karen. It hasn't always been easy, but it has been fun."

Karen said, "Not only have you really helped this company, I think you've made me and everyone else in this room better leaders."

"I'm not so sure that I have," Maria said; she just couldn't bring herself to accept the compliment.

"What do you mean?"

There had been something that had been bugging Maria recently. She had made great strides in getting the company and the executive team to embrace the Talent Management Principles. But there had been one more idea that had been nagging at Maria. She knew this probably wasn't the time or place to bring it up, but she just couldn't help herself. Keeping her mouth shut had never been one of her strengths, and being outspoken had served her well so far at Capital View, so she figured she would take one more shot.

"I've been wondering if we really have been good leaders."

"How can you say that?" Karen really didn't want to get into yet another argument with Maria, but couldn't she just accept a compliment and leave it at that? "The company has never been stronger. Profits are up, our employees are engaged like never before, and we're poised to have the best year in the company's history. Doesn't that indicate that we're pretty good at being leaders?"

"Not really," Maria answered. "I think all of that stuff indicates that we've been good managers."

"Let me guess," said Bobby. "Now you're going to educate all of us on the difference, right?"

Maria answered, "Well, as a matter of fact…"

Before she could finish, Bobby cut her off. "Since I have a feeling this might take a while, do you mind if I get a piece of cake before we start?"

Maria was always up for cake. "Bobby, I think that's the best idea you've had yet. Why don't we dive into this cake."

As the executive team dove into the cake, Maria dove into her idea. "Karen, you've just recited a nice list of business outcomes that we've achieved. That's terrific, but I don't think those accomplishments are evidence that we're good leaders. I think that makes us good managers."

"Isn't it the same thing?" asked Dave Marx.

"Not at all," Maria was just getting started. "There's a reason why they are two different words. Dave, what would you say is the job of a manager?"

"To manage people?" Dave asked without a lot of confidence.

"Yes, but why?"

"To get the job done, I guess." He figured he should sound more professional, so he amended it, "to achieve business results."

"Bingo. You've earned a second piece of cake. The job of the manager is to effectively achieve the organization's goals by efficiently using the organization's resources, both human and others."

Dave took her up on the offer for a second piece of cake. While he was getting it, he asked, "So doesn't that make us excellent leaders?"

"Not necessarily. Do you think it's possible to be a good manager without being a good leader?"

Will didn't want to see Dave put on the spot, so he decided to answer. "I suppose that if you tend to get results but always piss people off along the way, you can be seen as a good manager but a poor leader."

Maria continued her questioning. "And do you think it's possible to be a good leader without being a good manager."

"Sure." Will answered without having to give this one too much thought. "I have seen people in this organization who are exemplary leaders who are not even in managerial positions."

"So...?" Maria left this one open-ended.

"So leadership and management are two different things. I get that. But..." Will paused to make sure he phrased his next question carefully, "are you trying to tell us that we're bad leaders?"

"Not at all," Maria answered quickly. "I'm saying that the company's good results are a result of good management—by us and others. But simply getting good results does not make us leaders."

"So what does? Tell me, Maria, because I want to be a good leader," said Bobby, only half-joking.

"Well, what does it mean to be a good leader?" Maria recalled her discussion a few months ago with Ed Eddington about his leadership development program.

She wondered if this conversation would follow the same path.

"Ooh, ooh, I know this one," Bobby said, raising his hand and acting like an excited schoolchild. "A good leader is someone who has followers."

Maria played along. "A gold star for you, young man."

"But Dave got a second piece of cake."

"OK, Bobby, you can have a second piece."

"Good, because I want to grab that before I ask my next question. I'm afraid you'll take away my gold star after I ask it."

"Go ahead."

"We're the executive team of this company. All of our employees do what we say. Doesn't that make us leaders?"

"Why do you think they do what we say?"

"Because they know Karen would want to fire them if they didn't!"

"Hey, I'm not that bad," Karen said.

"Really, Bobby," Maria asked again, "why do our employees do what we say?"

"I guess it's because we're the executive team," he said. "We're their bosses."

"Right. It doesn't make us good leaders if people do what we say because of our positional authority."

"So what does make for good leadership?" Bobby said.

"You tell me," Maria responded. "Tell me what you think of when you think of great leadership?"

"The first thing that comes to my mind," Bobby answered, "is Martin Luther King. He had a vision, he communicated it well, and he got people to follow him."

"Did they follow him because they had to?"

"No. They followed him because they wanted to."

"I think that's a crucial difference. People here might do what we say even if they think it's a bad idea, because we're at the top of the org chart and it's their job to do what we say."

Will intervened. "I would hope they would push back if they thought we were asking them to do something that was a bad idea."

"Yes," Maria agreed, "and that's especially true if we as leaders have created a climate in which people can push back and disagree with us without fear of retribution."

Bobby was still chewing on this. "But we can't all be Martin Luther King."

"Right. Can you think of any other examples of great leadership?"

To Maria's surprise, it was Karen who not only responded, but gave the answer Maria was looking for. "I see great leadership here at Capital View all the time. When I send consulting teams out to clients, I frequently see one of the junior consultants emerge as the leader of the team."

"How do they do that?"

"They come up with good ideas and convince the other members of the team that it's a good idea and should be implemented. Then they influence the client to accept the ideas."

"Sounds like leadership to me. And it has nothing to do with their positional authority or where they are located on the org chart, does it?" asked Maria.

"Not at all."

"So Maria, are you suggesting that people at the top of the organization can't be leaders because our employees are obligated to do what we say?"

"I got this, Maria." Karen intercepted the question before Maria could answer. "No, Bobby, that's not what Maria and I are saying." She gave Maria a conspiratorial wink.

Maria loved it that Karen was taking the lead in a people discussion. Perhaps I really have made a difference in my first year at this company, Maria mused.

Karen continued, "I see excellent leadership from managers in my division all the time. Rather than giving orders, they discuss options with their people. Even when they do know what they want people to do, they ask nicely and say 'please' rather than giving orders."

Dave Marx jumped in. "I may be old school, but when a boss needs something done, why does he need to ask nicely and say please and thank you? When I was in the Army…"

Karen interrupted, "Dave, this isn't the military. People aren't legally obligated to follow our orders and we can't court martial them if they don't."

"Yeah, but we can fire them." Dave said.

"I'll tell you what," Bobby said, "if I fired everyone who didn't obey my orders, I would be awfully lonely."

Karen said, "One thing I've learned about management—especially over the past year," she gave Maria a friendly smile, "is that people are a lot more likely to do their best work if they want to do what we're asking. If we give orders, they might follow the order, but only give the minimum effort to get the job done. If they really believe in what they're doing, they're much more likely to give discretionary effort and go the extra mile. That's how you get excellent performance from our people."

I couldn't have said it better myself, thought Maria.

"So bottom-line it for me." Bobby was addressing Karen, not Maria.

"Leadership isn't about getting people to follow your orders. It's about getting people to buy into your vision and believe in what you're doing."

"I'm still dying to know," Bobby asked, "are we good leaders or not?"

"It depends," said Karen thoughtfully, "on whether our people really believe in the changes we've been asking them to make, or if they're just doing what we ask because they have to in order to keep their jobs."

It was time for Maria to rejoin the conversation. "From what I've observed, I think our people really do respect this executive team. And not to sound like I'm sucking up to the boss, I think Will has been an exemplary leader of this team and he is perceived by our people to be a great leader of this organization. Will, I think you've earned the respect of most of the people in this organization and that they are willing to follow you, not because you're the CEO, but because they believe in you. That, to me, is excellent leadership."

"Thanks for the compliment," Will said, looking at his watch and noticing that it was 4:55, "but it's been a long day, a long week, and," he looked at Maria with a big grin, "a long year. Can you or your new buddy Karen tell us the Talent Management Principle so we can all finally get out of here?"

Karen turned to Maria, "I guess I'll let you field this one."

"Thanks, Karen." Maria turned to Will.

Talent Management Principle Number 13

Being at the top of an organization does not make someone a leader. Positional authority makes you a manager; leaders can be anywhere in an organization. Delivering results makes you a good manager; getting people to willingly follow you makes you a good leader.

"Thanks, Maria," Will said in concluding the meeting. "You've certainly given us all a lot to think about today—and throughout this year. I look forward to seeing what you come up with in the next year."

Me too, thought Maria. She reflected on her first year on the job. She had shared her 13 Talent Management Principles with the organization. She had gotten Karen Michaels to embrace her way of thinking about people. Overall, she was proud of what she had accomplished during her first year at the company. She knew that Capital View really had a competitive advantage simply by adopting the Talent Management Principles. She wished that every company practiced the principles as well as Capital View. Then again, if everyone did, there wouldn't be much of a need for people like her; and those few organizations that really manage talent well would no longer have a competitive advantage.

Organizational Assessment

	NOT AT ALL		NEUTRAL		TO A GREAT EXTENT
1. Does your organization avoid using the terms "management" and "leadership" interchangeably?	1	2	3	4	5
2. Do you consider the executives in your organization to be good managers?	1	2	3	4	5
3. Do you consider the executives in your organization to be good leaders?	1	2	3	4	5
4. Do the people in your organization tend to follow the executive team because they want to (out of respect for the executives and their vision) as opposed to following because they have to (based on positional authority)?	1	2	3	4	5
5. To what extent do you see excellent leadership demonstrated by people in your organization who are not in senior positions?	1	2	3	4	5
6. To what extent do you believe your organization practices the Talent Management Principles described in this book?	1	2	3	4	5
7. To what extent do you believe your organization will be practicing the Talent Management Principles one year from now?	1	2	3	4	5

Questions for Personal Reflection

1. Was there anything described in chapter 13 that seemed descriptive of your organization?

2. Do you consider yourself to be a good manager? If so, what are the strengths and skills that make you a good manager?

3. Do you consider yourself to be a good leader? If so, what strengths and skills contribute to your leadership abilities?

4. Now that you have finished this book, what can you do to ensure that your organization practices the Talent Management Principles more effectively?

5. And finally, now that you have finished this book, what specifically will you do differently in your job and career?

The Talent Management Principles

1. People are your organization's most valuable asset. Behave as if you believe this to be true every day.

2. The most important job of a manager is to oversee the talent in an organization. The best way to achieve results is to hire, develop, engage, and retain good people.

3. Having better people is the best source of competitive advantage, so attracting top talent is a top priority. Be willing to do whatever it takes to bring in top talent. Do not let your own policies prevent you from hiring exceptional people.

4. The job of manager requires specific skills and abilities. Promotion should be based on the ability to do the next job, not performance in the current job. Good performance should be rewarded appropriately, but promotion should not be a reward for past performance.

5. Employees are smart and know how to pursue rewards. If you want to see certain behaviors and results, hold employees accountable. It's irrational to expect employees to deliver outcomes if we do not hold them accountable.

6. If you're going to hold people accountable, you must provide clearly articulated, measurable standards. There is no accountability without measurement.

7. Money spent on training and development is not a cost, it's an investment—an investment designed to increase the asset value of our most valuable resource.

8. If you're going to treat training and development as an investment, then you must be able to demonstrate a return on that investment. That means that every program should be designed to deliver a specific business result and should be held accountable for achieving that result.

9. Your organization is full of creative people who are capable of generating new ideas. As an organization, you need to find ways to implement new ideas instead of inhibiting innovation. If the organization is not innovative, it's an organizational or cultural problem, not a people problem.

10. The wealth of an organization lies in the knowledge and skills residing in its people. The ability to manage, collect, and share that knowledge can be a competitive advantage and an opportunity to leverage value without bringing additional resources into the organization.

11. Having four different generations in the workforce is not a new problem. It's not new—there have always been workers in a wide range of ages working together. And it's not a problem—it's another form of diversity that can be a valuable asset if managed properly.

12. People tend to resist change, and this resistance is often based more on emotion than reason. Individual conversations can speed the change process more than making a business case. The successful implementation of change initiatives usually takes more time than you originally anticipate.

13. Being at the top of an organization does not make someone a leader. Positional authority makes you a manager; leaders can be anywhere in an organization. Delivering results makes you a good manager; getting people to willingly follow you makes you a good leader.

ABOUT THE AUTHOR

Mark Allen, PhD, is an educator, speaker, consultant, and author who specializes in talent management and corporate universities. Mark is a member of the faculty of Pepperdine University's Graziadio School of Business and Management, where he previously served for 10 years as director of executive education. He is also a senior associate with the Kiely Group, a senior faculty member of the Human Capital Institute, and has taught for Vatel University and the American Management Association. He is the author of several books including *The Next Generation of Corporate Universities* and *The Corporate University Handbook*. He has also written numerous articles in practitioner and academic publications.

As an internationally recognized authority, he is a popular speaker and has presented his research in numerous countries including China, France, Italy, Turkey, Mexico, and the United States. He has consulted with or delivered executive development programs for 3M, Alpha Natural Resources, AT&T, Boeing, Caesars, Farmers Insurance, Kaiser Permanente, the Los Angeles Police Department, Samsung, Southern California Edison, the government of Taiwan, Verizon, and many other global organizations. Previously, Mark worked at the University of Southern California's Marshall School of Business where he developed highly successful executive education programs. He has also held managerial positions at Kaplan, Integrated Data Concepts, and SRS Publishing.

Mark has a bachelor's degree in psychology from Columbia University, an MBA from Pepperdine University, and a PhD in education from USC. He lives in Redondo Beach, California, with his wife Dayna and their two sons, Skyler and Dylan.

Made in the USA
Lexington, KY
26 August 2014